BIRDS OF THE AIR

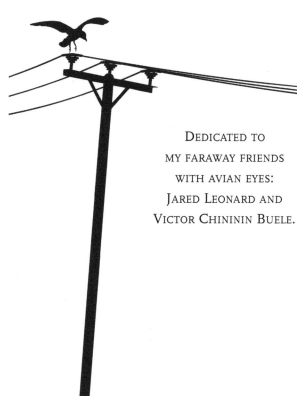

Dedicated to
my faraway friends
with avian eyes:
Jared Leonard and
Victor Chininin Buele.

Mike Bull is a graphic designer who lives and works in the Blue Mountains west of Sydney, Australia. His passion is understanding and teaching the Bible.

Also by this author:

Totus Christus: A Biblical Theology of the Whole Christ

Bible Matrix: An Introduction to the DNA of the Scriptures

Bible Matrix II: The Covenant Key

God's Kitchen: Theology You Can Eat & Drink

Reading the Bible in 3D

The Shape of Galatians: A Covenant-Literary Analysis

Sweet Counsel: Essays to Brighten The Eyes

Inquiétude: Essays for a People without Eyes

Birds of the air
THEOLOGICAL TWITTER

Copyright © 2016 Michael Bull

All rights reserved. No part of this book may be used or reproduced by any means, graphic, electronic, or mechanical, including photocopying, recording, taping or by any information storage retrieval system without the written permission of the publisher except in the case of brief quotations embodied in critical articles and reviews.

Unless otherwise indicated, all Scripture quotations are taken from *The Holy Bible, English Standard Version* copyright 2001 by Crossway Bibles, a publishing ministry of Good News Publishers. All rights reserved.

Because of the dynamic nature of the Internet, any web addresses or links contained in this book may have changed since publication and may no longer be valid. The views expressed in this work are solely those of the author and do not necessarily reflect the views of the publisher, and the publisher hereby disclaims any responsibility for them.

ISBN-13: 978-1541371941
ISBN-10: 1541371941

Designed and typeset by Michael Bull

INTRODUCTION
TWEETING SINCE THE DAWN OF TIME

RICHARD BAXTER famously exhorted Christians to screw the truth into the minds of their hearers and to thus work Christ into their affections. Baxter's exhortation is itself a perfect example of the *means* of such an exhortation. Who can hear these words and not be struck with the image of someone twisting a screwdriver in close proximity to somebody else's brain?

His use of the word "screw" communicates not only that effectively imparting truth is a *process* but also that it is *painful*. The truth will not change us until we actually *feel* it. Moreover, Baxter's image suggests that the darkened minds of human beings are as dense, stubborn and unresponsive as blocks of unseasoned wood. Delivering truth most often meets with some *resistance*.

A further and no less important observation is that a screw is a *tiny* instrument. Like a claw or a tooth, a screw is simply the spearhead of a larger tool. This makes it not less effective but more so. It concentrates, focuses, *magnifies* all of the blunt brute strength behind it into a single point. Most great men in history became great because they were compelled by a single truth, one expressed in so few words that it caught like a splinter in

BIRDS OF THE AIR

the flesh of the mind. Being both small *and* sharp it could not be ignored and thus allowed them no peace.

Yet there is one more facet of a screw that sets it apart from a simple nail. It has a thread which holds it in place, making it almost as much work to take out as it was to put in. The most effective delivery of truth is not necessarily the simplest. A screw must also be *tough*.

Bob Jones Sr. tells us that "Simplicity is truth's most becoming garb." However, this statement requires some qualification. A better choice of terminology might have been "the facts" rather than the word "truth." Jones' intended meaning is that deceivers (disguised as salespeople, teachers, politicians, scientists and theologians) employ complexity to obscure or mask the facts. That is darkness masquerading as an angel of light. But like God, enlightenment also comes wrapped in thick clouds. As Albert Einstein quipped, "God may be subtle but He's not malicious."

Paul condemned those who were "ever-learning," filling their minds with facts but never arriving at a knowledge of the truth. Are facts not true? What is the difference between a fact and a truth? Truth is composed of facts which exist *in relation to each other*, and thus is not simple. Facts are steps. Truth is a journey.

Oswald Chambers firmly believed in the concept of "seed thoughts" — brief, pithy sayings designed to arrest attention and stimulate thinking. He writes:

> Our Lord was never impatient. He simply planted seed thoughts in the disciples' minds and surrounded

TWEETING SINCE THE DAWN OF TIME

them with the atmosphere of His own life. We get impatient and take men by the scruff of the neck and say: "You must believe this and that." You cannot make a man see moral truth by persuading his intellect. "When He, the Spirit of truth is come, He shall guide you into all truth."[1]

In every sphere there are degrees of knowledge. Knowing something because you read about it and knowing it by experience are different levels of the same thing. This is why we struggle to learn from the mistakes of others.

Facts are dead elements. Truth is a living organism. Facts are things which we can collect and store, but the truth is something which possesses *us*. It cannot be caged and will not be pinned down. The modern scientistic mindset confuses the accumulation of facts with an understanding of the truth. Knowledge is not wisdom, which is why many well-intended government schemes go so horribly wrong.

Truth is transformative, something which causes us to grow and brings us to spiritual maturity. That is why animals can survive on food alone but human beings also require a steady diet of truth. Paul takes it even further, noting that spiritual maturity is a progression from milk to something that requires chewing. Spiritual nourishment is *work* because work makes us *strong*.

To change us, a truth must engage us, so it is often imparted in an enigma. The truth wrapped in a riddle or

[1] Oswald Chambers, *Run Today's Race: A Word from Oswald Chambers for Every Day of the Year,* December 9.

BIRDS OF THE AIR

a joke is irresistible. What looks like skylarking is sometimes the fowler's snare. When God speaks to us in veiled language, symbols, parables and even architecture, we are forced to contemplate, or ruminate, upon what He has said. In some cases, the meaning of certain Scriptures is still being debated, even after many centuries. But what we must realize is that *this was always the plan.*

The very first law given by God to humanity was itself a puzzle designed to provoke meditation and bring forth the fruit of wisdom. Jesus' own ministry, the testimony of the Man who declared Himself to be the light of the world, was anything but a "simple" delivery of the truth.

Our desire to speak the truth plainly is part of the reason why modern preaching mostly fails to engage its hearers. God's process is "word-and-response" so His true prophets are always provocative. Jesus was at the pointy end of a long line of troublemakers who trafficked in barbs, riddles and shocking object lessons. Instead of doling out rose water they went straight for the gasoline.

Those who indulge in murder and adultery are often the first to insist upon table manners, which is why God sends a Jeremiah to smash the pottery or an Isaiah to preach naked in the street. King Solomon might tell us that there is a time to be polite and a time to give some obstinate official a poke in the eye. Douglas Wilson writes:

> In a sinful world, giving offense is one of the central tasks of preaching. When the offending word is brought to bear against those who have shown themselves to be unteachable, they are written off by that offending word.

TWEETING SINCE THE DAWN OF TIME

When this happens, or there is a threat of it happening, the natural temptation is to blame the word instead of taking responsibility for the sin that brought the rebuking and satiric word. Employing a scriptural satiric bite is therefore not "rejoicing in iniquity" but rather testifying against hardness of heart.[2]

Like King Solomon and the other authors of the book of Proverbs, Jesus also understood the power in pastoral ministry of a well-timed and well-considered sound-bite. Toby Sumpter writes:

> I would defend the art of pastoral tweet bombing by pointing to the perfect pastor: Jesus Christ. He's the Head Pastor of the Church, the Chief Shepherd, and we take our cues from Him. Jesus invented Twitter. Jesus was the first pastor to employ Twitter in His pastoral ministry.
>
> He may not have had a smart phone or even a dumb phone, but Jesus was the master of throwing out short truths that were calculated to poke, prod, and offend.
>
> Here are a few samples from Matthew's Twitter Feed:
>
> "Follow Me, and let the dead bury their dead." (Mt. 8:22)
>
> "Those who are well have no need of a physician, but those who are sick. But go and learn what this means: 'I desire mercy and not sacrifice.' For I did not

---

[2] Douglas Wilson, *A Serrated Edge: A Brief Defense of Biblical Satire and Trinitarian Skylarking*, 102.

BIRDS OF THE AIR

come to call the righteous, but sinners to repentance." (Mt. 9:12-13)

"Do not think that I came to bring peace on earth. I did not come to bring peace but a sword." (Mt. 10:34)

"I have come to set a man against his father, a daughter against her mother, and a daughter-in-law against her mother-in-law." (Mt. 10:35)

"Take heed and beware of the leaven of the Pharisees." (Mt. 16:6)

"If you want to be perfect, go, sell what you have and give it to the poor, and you will have treasure in heaven, and come follow Me." (Mt. 19:21)

The point is that Jesus frequently said things in short, pointy ways that not only *could* be misunderstood, but which frequently were and were meant to be. Jesus didn't apologize and promise to only write essays, books, and give long sermons that explained everything more carefully. Jesus kept right on saying things that were startling, confusing, and could be easily misunderstood. In fact, Jesus ultimately was condemned for statements that were twisted and taken out of context.[3]

Although the aphorisms of Solomon and Jesus share the characteristic of brevity with most of what flies on Twitter, the difference — and power — lies in their ability to pack gravity into a grain of sand. A tweet with more impact than airborne poop takes time to consider and thus time to compose. Peter Leithart writes:

---

[3] Toby Sumpter, "In Defense of Pastoral Tweet Bombing," tobyjsumpter.com, April 25, 2012.

TWEETING SINCE THE DAWN OF TIME

I joined Twitter to keep track of my kids, and so I could bash their short attention spans. Then Pastor Douglas Wilson observed that tweets are like proverbs. You try to capture, in a haiku flash, some of the goodness and beauty of things. Doug was right: Now they're faster and there's more of them, and more that are useless, but folks have been tweeting since the dawn of time.[4]

The Proverbs were no doubt designed to be read aloud either at court or in the congregation, and a moment of silence, a mental breather, like the "musical rest" of the original Sabbath, would be necessary after each to allow time for meditation. I make this speculation because there is a danger in reading Proverbs as though it were a book of prose. Doing so — to turn upside-down Luther's analogy concerning sinful thoughts — allows birds to fly overhead which were specially created to nest in our hair.

One tweet per page would facilitate such rests in what follows here, but since that would be impractical, I will trust you to give each its intended Sabbath. Hopefully they are stimulating or provocative enough to give you pause all on their own.

Michael Bull
December 2016

---

[4] Peter Leithart, "Bashing Twitter's Bashers," firstthings.com, January 21, 2014.

"Atheism is a crutch for those who cannot bear the reality of God."

— TOM STOPPARD

CREATION

#1
Whenever the Word of God comes,
it is an end to business as usual.

#2
The pen is mightier than the sword because
Word always comes before Sacrament.

#3
The Bible's literary labyrinth radiates organically from
an algorithm so simple it can be grasped by a child.

#4
There is a heavenly breath and an earthly breath.
Between them is one who possesses both
as mediator between heaven and earth.

#5
The first union of heaven and earth was an illegal one.
It was the possession of an animal
by an angel with grand designs.

#6
The serpent was a king composed "before God's time,"
a false Shekinah intending to usurp Adam's priestly rule.

#7
There is no chaos in Genesis 1, only emptiness.
Chaos is the result of the original sin.

BIRDS OF THE AIR

#8
Evolutionary theory is the Alchemy of modern science.

#9
Computer-modeled "extrapolations" based on a flawed
worldview always create a fantasy world
as they do with evolution and climate science.

#10
A theory does not transform data into evidence.

#11
The biggest lie of atheism is that it is religiously neutral.

#12
The Transcendent God has always seen right through us.
Now in Christ, we can see right through Him.

#13
Adam and Eve's "physical" eyes were opened
well before their "ethical" eyes were opened.

#14
Spiritually-speaking, we are all Eve, all "women caught in
adultery," yet Jesus speaks to us as a better Adam.

#15
Those willing to believe that Abram and Jacob
were deceivers rather than discerners are as
dumb as Adam before the serpent.

CREATION

#16
There is no world peace without the Spirit of Christ.
We are all sinners, and like poles repel.

#17
Psalm 1 and the Revelation share a similar structure
because both are about The Blessed Man.

#18
The theologian who "proves" with the parables that Genesis
1-3 is only poetry is illiterate, illogical, and ill-informed.

#19
Any attempt to shift the foundations of the Bible is to play
Jenga with Covenant history, which is a carefully
constructed tower to heaven.

#20
Why does Twitter keep suggesting atheists for me to follow?
Does Twitter think I don't know where they are going?

#21
In the light of the Bible Matrix even the best theology
is little better than a pile of straw bricks.
God gives us His word as architecture.

#22
Adam's failure to discern a veiled blessing in the
prohibitions of God was passed on to all his children.

BIRDS OF THE AIR

#23
Adam's sin, like Israel's, was desiring
kingdom before God's time.

#24
God's answer to the Fall was not abortion but adoption.

#25
We have grown so accustomed to the Bible that we have
forgotten how astonishingly eccentric it is.

#26
Theistic evolution's desire to marry faith and evolution
is as ill-conceived as that of atheists to divorce faith
from empirical science.

#27
The scientific establishment has never been fundamentally
wrong until proven fundamentally wrong.

#28
"We are the ones we've been waiting for?" No.
Jesus, a better Adam, is the "we" we were waiting for:
holy, meek, inspired and steadfast.

#29
As it was for Adam, the first step towards inheriting the
earth is to be faithful in the day of small things.

#30
Adam was the first liberal theologian.

CREATION

#31
Scientists are welcome in the Church. But the phallus
of scientism must not be set up in the Sanctuary.

#32
According to evolutionary theory, death created life.
According to evolutionary theory, distortions created beauty.

#33
The first person to shift blame was Adam,
and the second to shift blame was God Himself.

#34
All our actions have consequences
for which we are held accountable because
we were made in the image of a consequential God.

#35
In the Garden, Adam named the beasts.
At the cross, the beasts named Adam.

#36
If there is no Father in heaven, there can be
no fathers on earth. The state becomes a goddess,
a surrogate parent, and a single parent.

#37
Modern man rewrote his origin
that he might be master of his own destiny.

BIRDS OF THE AIR

#38
The Bible: "The heavens declare the glory of God..."
Man: "You didn't build that!"*

#39
For neo-Darwinism, climate science and modern social theory, peer review means getting your friends to mark your papers.

#40
Atheism's historical revisionism begins with the reclassification of chaos as holy Cause rather than unholy Effect.

#41
It takes only one miracle to prove that the so-called natural order is not a closed system.

#42
Adam was supposed to obey not because of what he knew but because of what he knew of his Father. This also explains the end of Job.

#43
Science cuts things up and tells us what they are made of, but its scope is limited when it comes to telling us what they are actually for.

---

*A reference to President Obama's statement in 2012 that building a successful business depends upon government investment, implying that the state should receive in taxation a greater share of the rewards of entrepreneurship, innovation and hard work.

CREATION

#44
The voice of slain Abel was a red spring rising up from the ground which made Cain's Land barren (Gen. 2:6; 4:9-12).

#45
Evolution is a car with no engine, that leaves no tracks and that no one has ever actually seen.

#46
As in Eden, the exemplary love of the Man would lead to the empowerment of Woman as co-regent.

#47
Science is always a gift from God. It should be no surprise when Man turns it into an idol that speaks.

#48
If you can believe pond scum can accidentally turn into people, you can believe anything.

#49
An encounter with God changes you.
He is not known by observation but by experience as with any relationship.

#50
An atheist telling you all about religion is like a cat telling you all about surfing.

#51
If His words are rejected, God deliberately hides Himself from the disobedient.

BIRDS OF THE AIR

#52
You are not the product of blind chance.
Your metanarrative is invalid.

#53
The defeat of the serpent required the completion
of the Triune Office in a single man.

#54
Because God can only be truly known through
obedient faith, sinful man wants a God who can be known
entirely through scientific observation.

#55
The secular identification of the Bible as the problem is
akin to Israel's identification of Moses as the problem.

#56
A truly biblical worldview is not one in which
the interpreter provides the appropriate lens:
the text itself is the lens.

#57
Old Earth Creationism is like the Star Wars prequels.
You know it happened, but there's no way it was that bad.

#58
Why is Bible chronology never the primary source?
It gets judged in the "light" of arguments
fabricated from fragments.

CREATION

#59
God gives glory to the Man when he sees
the glory as nothing and God as everything.

#60
If there is indeed any ecological lesson from Noah's story,
it is that the earth can be abundant only through
a faithful Man blessed by God.

#61
The serpent was the first household god.

#62
The first "expert" was the serpent in the Garden.

#63
Only a talking snake will tell you that
a talking snake is an impossibility.

#64
The very first TED talk
is recorded for us in Genesis 3.

#65
Satan doesn't "steeple" his fingers like worldly
thought leaders. He Babels them.

#66
A dragon is a "corporate" serpent,
a body gathered to "incarnate" a lie.

BIRDS OF THE AIR

#67
Like Abraham, Adam was called to offer his
firstborn son, not to God but to the original Molech.

#68
"The universe is always sending me little messages..."
Yep. It's "You're going to die" on a loop.

#69
Covenant Creationism is the bastard homunculus
offspring of preterism and theistic evolution.

#70
Atheists reject all miracles, except for abiogenesis,
genetic information, and punctuated equilibrium.

#71
Since the Bible follows repeated patterns,
the reason for the two resurrections in Revelation
is found in the architecture of Genesis.

#72
The Torah was shaped by Ancient Near Eastern
cultures to the degree that a jello mold
is shaped by the jello.

#73
Noah curses Canaan and only two chapters later
God is already giving Canaan's stuff to Shem.

CREATION

#74
If Adam had conquered the tongue of the shining one,
his words would have been a flaming sword.

#75
A seraph is a fiery dragon from heaven – glory.
The serpent was a shining dragon on earth –
merely a reflected glory.

#76
In Noah's day, the world was not filled with
anarchical violence but the 70x7 unforgiving,
merciless vengeance established by Lamech.

#77
A son of man represents earth in heaven.
A son of God represents heaven on earth.

#78
It's not that I hate Christian academics who don't
believe Genesis. I just think they are devils who
should be publicly beaten with rods.

#79
Give me a dispensationalist who believes Genesis
over an amillennialist who doesn't, any day.

#80
My Covenant Renewal Worship friends can rest easy.
We in the Asia-Pacific have already renewed
the Covenant today.

BIRDS OF THE AIR

#81
The Bible doesn't seem to care at all about
Calvinism/Arminianism.

#82
In a universe of types and symbols, everything is
self-effacing. Everything speaks of something else,
and points us to the Perfect Unself.

#83
It's telling that the actual process of Creation
was nothing like the chaos of a big bang and
very much like an orderly worship service.

#84
How can we lock the God who inspired the very human
process of writing the Scriptures out of the very human
process of assembling the Canon?

#85
In the Bible, God deals with the world in fractals,
in layers, in types. This shouldn't surprise us.
This is how the world is built.

#86
Every moral choice echoes Eden. We are presented
with life disguised as death and death disguised as life
with only the Word as the key.

CREATION

#87
When God lines up animals He says, "This is your future" (Adam, Noah, Peter). When Darwin lines up animals, he says "This is your past."

#88
Intelligent design is easily refuted by showing a specific, fully-articulated Darwinian pathway for a complex system. But no one's done it.

#89
Any attempt to take any part of the text of Genesis 1-11 as non-historical requires some level of either dishonesty or self-deception.

#90
It doesn't matter if the science is illegitimate as long as it's consensual.

#91
Atheists, for whom life has no inherent purpose, arrogantly assume the role of giving it a purpose of their own devising.

#92
BioLogos: a bunch of old men educated in compromised, dying academies, who think death is good and will all be dead soon. Amen.

BIRDS OF THE AIR

#93
The events of Genesis chapters 1-3 are a triune architecture, working through Being, Knowing and Doing, or Word, Sacrament and Government.

#94
The characters and events in Genesis are the beginnings of long and colorful narrative threads.

#95
If Creationism makes the Church looks foolish, Theistic Evolutionism makes it look spineless and irrelevant.

#96
Enduring BioLogos videos is like listening to men who should know better hammering a square peg into a round hole.

#97
Theistic evolution has no balls. Where did the Seed come from if Adam's testicles are a myth?

#98
When Jesus refers to Himself as the Son of "Man," read it as Son of Adam, the promised Seed.

#99
As seeds in a fruit, blessing and cursing, eternity and destruction did God sow in Adam's heart.

CREATION

#100
If Adam had crushed the serpent and presented Eve
to God "chaste," she would truly have been his glory,
"the righteousness of God in him."

#101
Genesis begins with a serpent and a rainbow. It ends with a
man robed in a rainbow and then crowned with a serpent.

#102
Judgment is simply the light shining into the darkness.
History will end as it began, only more glorious.

#103
A call for the Church to focus on the environment
instead of the Gospel is to worry about a temporary
set at the expense of eternal actors.

#104
Do I believe in life on other planets? No.
The Spirit only hovered over this one. New life comes
by Covenant faithfulness. (Matthew 3:16-17)

#105
When God slew animals to cover Adam,
they became his glory and he became their life.

#106
In Genesis 48:14, Jacob's optic chiasm
is expressed with his arms.

BIRDS OF THE AIR

#107
Adams picture the beauty of self-sacrifice, but it is fitting that Eves picture grace and forgiveness, which are even more beautiful.

#108
Every step of history, personal or corporate, is a "Creation week." There is forming and filling, then blessing or cursing.

#109
The modern mind struggles with Genesis because it is multi-disciplinary: science, history, liturgy and poetry as one pan galactic cocktail.

#110
Eve "looked on" the skin, the glorious covering of the fruit. The sons of God looked on the glorious fruit of ungodly men.

#111
Forbidden fruit: seed, flesh and skin. The Garden sin split the seed, the Land split the flesh, and the World split the skin (uncovering).

#112
Adam was supposed to produce fruit, not steal it. Every sin is stealing something now that God promised to give us as a gift later.

CREATION

#113
Designing a machine to smash existing matter into bits as close to nothing as possible won't tell you how nothing turned into something.

#114
Atheism: the annoying kid who turned up late, brought nothing for the table, ridiculed everyone and ruined the party.

#115
The children of the free thinkers seem incapable of an original thought.

#116
Why is it that the people who risk their eternal destiny on the fact that they have opposable thumbs are the least likely to text you back?

#117
"The Gardening Bible," "The MYOB Bible," "The Golf Bible." Somebody should write "The Bible Bible."

#118
God's use of fractals in creation makes systems very efficient. Teaching the Bible's "fractals" makes that teaching very efficient also.

#119
If there is no God, you are just nature's way of keeping meat fresh.

BIRDS OF THE AIR

#120
If Adam and Eve were clothed in skins of bull and goats respectively, it would have been fitting for Adam to have worn the bloodied horns.

#121
In case it comes up, St. Augustine expressly taught that the world was 6,000 years old (City of God, Book XII, chapter 12).

#122
In Genesis 1, Adam is created a Priest. In Genesis 2, he is exalted as King. In Genesis 3, he is called to be a Prophet.

#123
Why do atheists get to decide what counts as evidence for God? 1) He says their faculties are dead and 2) He deliberately hides from them.

#124
One day, perhaps in a century or two, the word "Scientist" will be a term of derogation used to describe the cultists of the 20th century.

#125
Darwinism didn't only rewrite history, it usurped the intended purpose of homology. Animals mediated for sinful men.

CREATION

#126
Naturalism is akin to claiming that the working processes in an automobile are sufficient evidence of its self-construction.

#127
The world is necessarily a place of consequences – dire or sublime – because it is Trinitarian. Word requires Response.

#128
Adam was given an opportunity to fulfill his representation of God by dividing light from darkness with his own words.

#129
God allows false doctrine to divide the Church for the same reason He allowed the serpent into the Garden: our maturity and purification.

#130
Theological error is what drives theological advancement.

#131
The Bride doesn't hear directly from God but from the Bridegroom. She proclaims the crushing of the serpent OUTSIDE the Sanctuary.

#132
In the beginning, Adam was with God. All things on earth were to be made through him. He was to overcome darkness and be the light of men.

BIRDS OF THE AIR

#133
Adam was made of dust (presumably in the Land)
and placed into the Sanctuary. That makes him
the very first Firstfruits offering.

#134
Love is death. Adam is the firstfruits tithe.
Love is a miracle. Eve is the abundant harvest.

#135
The story from Adam to Noah is a Tabernacle: cruciform.
The waters of the flood flow from the Man's belly
(John 7:38, 19:34).

#136
All worldviews lay claim to some level of reason and logic.
The real issue is the fundamental assumptions
upon which these are based.

#137
If, when the Word became human flesh,
He had had to start out as primeval soup, we would
still be waiting for Christmas.

#138
Atheism claims empirical science to be its authority, but in
reality, it just rejects the Bible in favor of its own storybooks.

#139
The most potent and yet most misunderstood
form of promise in the Scriptures is sacred architecture,
beginning in Genesis 1.

CREATION

#140
If Creation and the Bible are anything to go by,
God isn't boring. It is theologians who are boring.

#141
When a theologian tells you to read Genesis
from an ANE perspective, he is actually telling you
Genesis is primitive and mistaken.*

#142
When Richard Dawkins stands before God,
he will wish He was a flying spaghetti monster.

#143
A true miracle is like God. It has no history of
"development" that we can trace. It just "is."

#144
Any analysis of history with Christ and His Church
as an artifact of it rather than the reason for it all
is going to misinterpret it.

#145
The history of time is what happens when
God temporarily puts eternity on hold.

#146
The world God made was good. Yet Adam's job was to make
the world a better place. That hasn't changed. Go to it.

---

*Many modern scholars believe Genesis was a story written to serve as a polemic against other cultures of the Ancient Near East. This subtly undermines its authority. Internal evidence indicates that its earlier chapters originated long before the rise of ANE culture, and were thus not composed but only *compiled* by Moses.

BIRDS OF THE AIR

#147
Both the living and written words are image bearers.

#148
Since naturalism by definition excludes miraculous supernatural causes, naturalists are forced to believe in miraculous natural causes.

#149
Evidence for God's existence is not found primarily in heaven or earth but in the one who fashioned the microscope and telescope: His image.

#150
Why did the prophets use "creation" language to describe "social" judgments? Because God saw the whole world in Israel.

#151
The doctrine of evolution is a subtle hybrid of the worship of beasts and the worship of ancestors. The serpent is its father.

#152
If Abel was merely a character in a myth given to us by God, why did God incarnate say that his blood needed to be avenged?

#153
The BioLogos boffins tell us how ancients understood Genesis, yet they reject the testimony of every ancient in the Bible, including Jesus.

CREATION

#154
Which Edenic tree does the cross represent?
Neither. And both.

#155
The first one to ever "bite the dust"
was the serpent in Eden.

#156
There's a subtle but crucial difference between
identifying a text's genre to better submit to the Word
and using genre to evade the Word.

#157
The "groaning" of the Christian and the Creation
is the aching of Forms desiring to be Filled.

#158
Sometimes, reading the Bible feels like
eavesdropping on a conversation between
the Father and the Son in the Spirit.

#159
You are not "made of stardust."
You are made of ordinary dust, and it was created
3 days before the stars even existed.

#160
The fractalline DNA of the Bible means that it is
self-correcting, self-governing. The Word itself has
the "internal law" of the Spirit.

BIRDS OF THE AIR

#161
In God's world, every journey begins with
a single step – on some reptile's head.

#162
Claiming that the earliest circumcisions were Egyptian
is as errant as claiming the earliest Covenants were Hittite.
Give God some credit.

#163
The first Adam killed everyone.
The last Adam was killed by everyone.

#164
The Bible rarely deals with the abstract,
and when it does, it uses decidedly earthy symbols.
The earth is heaven expounded.

#165
Christians who reject a talking snake must also deal with
the talking donkey. Animals are earthly angels.

#166
Theology divorced from narrative is gnosticism.
"Story" divorced from theology is rebellion. Heaven and
earth are forever bound by Covenant.

#167
Genesis begins and ends with blessings and curses revealed
to a young man who is put in charge of the food.

CREATION

#168
Every line of Genesis 1-3 is a seed.
And every stanza of Genesis 4-50 is a sapling.

#169
The Bible has no vestigial organs.
It is the modern theologian which has lost all or most of its original function through evolution.

#170
Modern theology has misclassified most of the Bible as junk DNA. As with junk DNA, it's simply because they don't yet know what it's for.

#171
Rejoicing with Sagan because "everything is made of stardust" is akin to amazement on discovering that all words are made of letters.

#172
Atheism's demand for impersonal evidence of God results from the rejection of the legal testimony of a specific Person.

#173
The sin of humanity is the sin of Adam, which is the unwillingness to believe that God is good.

#174
We know there isn't a flying spaghetti monster because that is not the image in which we were made.

BIRDS OF THE AIR

#175
As it was in the days of Noah, stay faithful because
your vindication will come in torrents.

#176
Genesis is not a response to the religious situation
of the day. And Revelation is not a response to the
political situation of the day.

#177
"All religions are equal, except atheism,
which is more equal than other religions."
– The Pigs

#178
The entire Bible was written in one language: image.

#179
Adam faced a serpent in the Garden.
Christ faced the serpent in the Garden,
his cohorts in the Land, and his armies in the World.

#180
The fruitfulness of the earth is sourced in its
submission to the governing lights.

#181
As with Abraham, God's household in heaven
was a tent of servants, but there was only one Son,
through whom came all Creation.

"I guess I work best when my heart is broken."
— TIM PAGE

DIVISION

#182
God's ways are often mysterious to us because they involve movements from invisible to visible and vice versa.

#183
The stewardship delegated by any Covenant is historical. It has a definite beginning and a definite end.

#184
Covenant authority shelters a Man while God trains him to become a shelter for others.

#185
Before Abraham, sacrifices were whole burnt offerings because there was no "division of flesh."

#186
Before Moses, the animals were only cut in half, because there were no Levitical priests serving as purifying organs in the body.

#187
Before Christ, only animals served as sacrificial substitutes, because no man was blameless without the shedding of blameless blood.

#188
Coercion forms us when we are immature.
Submission fills us when we are mature.
Here is the first Adam and the Last.

BIRDS OF THE AIR

#189
God's people are never cornered. They are simply bait to bring Pharaoh out of Egypt to his destruction.

#190
Circumcision promised physical seed.
Baptism celebrates spiritual fruit.

#191
For Israel, "taking the Lord's name in vain" meant publicly joining His team and flying His flag but then playing for the other side.

#192
The difference between Passover and the Lord's Supper is the difference between the table in Exodus 12 and the one in Exodus 24.

#193
In biblical history, there was never a Covenant sign upon children, but upon males and upon professing believers.

#194
Sorrow for sin is a gift from heaven. It is a sign of your adoption into the eternal family.

#195
God is a libertarian, but unlike the earthly variety, He knows the difference between true freedom and slavery to sin disguised as freedom.

DIVISION

#196
In His circumcision, Jesus was the "Son of 'the Beloved'" (David) and in His baptism He was the "Beloved Son."

#197
Covenant theology is great.
New Covenant theology is greater.

#198
"Holy" means "integrated" and also "set apart."
So it means separate and together all at once,
just like the Church.

#199
In the Church, as in our culture, we either neglect to train our children or we overcompensate and turn our children into idols.

#200
The difference between raising a son
and raising a daughter is a bit like that between
herding cattle and growing flowers.

#201
When you kick the Spirit of God out of education,
other spirits fill the vacuum.

#202
Praying, reading the Bible to your kids, and being hospitable, are simple solutions to big problems.
But simple is too humbling.

BIRDS OF THE AIR

#203
Humble pie is always fresh.

#204
Classical Music used to be called music.
Classical Education used to be called education.

#205
Where they disagree, the Bible scrubs the floor
with church tradition.

#206
Tradition is nothing but a pedestal for the truth.
Too many Christians gather around empty pedestals.

#207
Because of the promise to Adam and to Abraham, even in
death Israel was always a seed planted in the ground.

#208
If your work polarizes people, that's a good sign
it has a future. Separating sheep from goats
is always the way forward.

#209
As a "human shield," a firmament of flesh,
the office of Mediator is a position of passivity
towards God and activity towards Creation.

DIVISION

#210
Writing theology has all the tension of the
Sistine Chapel: it is backbreaking yet glorious,
and must please both the heavens and the earth.

#211
The ancients hid things in esoterica to maintain power.
God hides things so we will seek Him and be empowered.

#212
Israel's circumcision of flesh began in Abraham and
ended at Passover. Israel's circumcision of heart
began in Moses and ended at Jericho.

#213
God kept His people in Egypt from intermarriage, yet they
committed harlotry in their hearts with Egypt's gods.

#214
The plagues at the hands of Aaron and Moses
were a repossession of the prosperity
brought by Joseph as God's right hand.

#215
If the Bible's circumcision and virginity tokens
are barbaric, how can infanticide and treating
virginity like a token be progressive?

#216
The heart of typology is representation,
and representation is the heart of sacrifice.

BIRDS OF THE AIR

#217
Paedobaptism is an attempt to claim Abrahamic promises in a post-Abrahamic world.

#218
The mark on Cain preserved his life until a man, Noah, was qualified to judge. Just so, the circumcision was a mark on Man until Christ.

#219
Jesus covered our sins by wearing them. When I am sinned against, am I willing to wear it?

#220
Both Joseph and Jesus wore stripes.

#221
The essence of death isn't cessation, but neither is it separation as many believe. It is scattering.

#222
To believe in Apostolic Succession, one has to misunderstand both "apostolic" and "succession."

#223
Ichabod is now written over every public school.

#224
Academia gives us a dusty box full of lenses to help us to read the Bible, all the while ignoring the fact that the Bible is our lens.

DIVISION

#225
When the Lord passes over, the sons become slaves and the slaves become sons.

#226
The New Covenant is objective, but what is its object? The believer? The Church? No. The entire world.

#227
Jeroboam's golden calves were skinny Egyptian cows with full tummies.

#228
Being in awe of Aslan is better than being enthralled by Captain America, but the Bible itself gives us scores of far better images of Jesus.

#229
For Dagon to be dismembered, the Tabernacle of God must always be dismembered first.

#230
Words are swords. They are made to cut something, even when they are intended to build up and edify.

#231
The fact that there are blackbirds and white birds in Genesis 15 reminds us that the Circumcision prevented another global flood.

BIRDS OF THE AIR

#232
The generation consistently exhorted as children to
"follow its heart" is totally lacking in discernment.

#233
The "children of God" are conceived by hearing
the seed of the Word. (Mark 4:14)

#234
The "children" of Jesus are too big to re-enter the womb.
(John 3:4; Hebrews 2:13)

#235
A Church with no concern for its lack of
serious Bible teaching is a train off the tracks.
Movement without direction is worthless.

#236
In the TORAH and the prophets, it is not God
who is bloodthirsty. It is sin that is bloodthirsty.

#237
Is contraception a sin? A better question is this:
Are children a blessing or a curse?

#238
What is a dragon? A serpent whose legs have grown back.

#239
Revelation is every Bible story rolled into one.
If we recognize Jesus "passing over" the churches in 2-3,
we can understand what follows.

DIVISION

#240
Israel was a new body constructed upon the bones of Joseph. Unlike the prodigal, Joseph left Canaan empty and came back full.

#241
Circumcision was a division of flesh on earth (blood). Baptism mediates between heaven and earth (water).

#242
The Tabernacle wasn't a museum of static truths. It was a detailed anatomy of the to-and-fro between Father and Son, and heaven and earth.

#243
The heart of the New Covenant is not raising children but plundering and recruiting the heirs of the pagans as soldiers for Christ.

#244
"'No' and 'Dad' are two words that don't go together. Unless I'm asking you to rob a bank. Got it?"

#245
Since even the OT differentiates between circumcision of flesh (Abraham) and circumcision of heart (Moses), why would the NT confuse them?

#246
The Covenant with David was a cut within Moses, which was a cut within Abraham, which was a cut within Noah, which was a cut within Adam.

BIRDS OF THE AIR

#247
A Covenant is an education, so it requires
a childlike faith. But its goal is adulthood,
self-government, internal government by the Spirit.

#248
I wish a thick skin didn't have to be scar tissue.

#249
When you break bread – with your Ten Fingers –
remember Jesus' body under the Law of Moses.

#250
AD66 Jesus: "You want circumcision? You've got it."
The Roman armies cut a trench around Jerusalem,
built a wall, and crucified Jews on it.

#251
A blunt sermon usually comes from
the sharpest knife in the block.

#252
The Gospel and the parables are designed to
polarize people. Once you hear them, you start
heading north or south.

#253
The Bible contains many "hidden things," but there
are no eternal mysteries. Every veil will be torn.

DIVISION

#254
Animal sacrifice: the redemption of a kingly son
with the blood of a priestly servant.

#255
The blood type on the Shroud of Turin is the rare AB –
The Universal Recipient.

#256
God takes the firstborn. Abel offered a substitute for Cain
on the altar. Cain didn't like being a living sacrifice.

#257
A Jew-Gentile World conspired against a Jew-Gentile
Church, two offspring fighting in the womb while
birthpangs ripped the old world apart.

#258
The source of all inequality in the world, and its remedy,
are found in the relationship between the Father
and the Son by the Spirit.

#259
Mary's birth pangs heralded the 1st Christmas.
What did the birth pangs in the AD60s herald?
(Matthew 24:8) Jew and Gentile in one new man.

#260
After his anointing to judge Israel, Jehu's men
put their garments at his feet. After Stephen's murder,
Paul's followers did the same.

BIRDS OF THE AIR

#261
The Law was cut into stones and given to Moses,
but the promise was cut into the stones of Abraham.

#262
Sadly, the only foreign land in which modern
Christians sojourn is the Bible. God's landscape and
customs are entirely alien to us.

#263
For Abraham, the nakedness of circumcision led
to his "clothing" with offspring, a glory robe.
He pictured the Day of Atonement (John 8:56)

#264
Abel was a keeper of sheep. Cain asked if he was his
brother's keeper to cover slaying him like a sheep.

#265
Cain "opened the womb," but
he was a firstborn that was not God's.

#266
Revelation presupposes a veil.

#267
"Wake up
O sleeper
Rise
From the dead
And Christ
On you
Will shine."

*"What one secretly hopes from a reader is:
I always knew that but never realized it before.
Then you know what you've said is true."*

— W. H. Auden

ASCENSION

#268
The twin tablets in the Ark were the sentence of death,
the naked, earthen bodies of Adam and Eve
slain without mercy in the Sanctuary.

#269
Moses deals with the animal.
Christ deals with the *animus*.

#270
Claiming that the Church is necessary for salvation is like
claiming that a flock is necessary to be a sheep.

#271
Tip: If a church goes through many hired pastors,
the church is the problem. If it's the other way around,
the pastor is the problem.

#272
I hope the resurrection includes animals.
I mean, what we gonna eat?

#273
Ruth: a Moabitess (daughter of Lot; refused Israel food)
who made Israel fruitful again after a famine.
Think about that one for a bit.

#274
Replacement theology? No. Consumption theology.
Christ fulfilled Israel, so the Church consumes
Israel every week.

BIRDS OF THE AIR

#275
The Bible is not grain which needs the cultural husk
removed to glean the timeless truths.
It is already bread and wine, a readied feast.

#276
Under Moses, the law was written on tablets
that it might be written on flesh. Under Christ,
the opposite is true. Theonomy is within you.

#277
Passover separated Israel from Egypt, but the Law
separated Levites from Israel. Likewise, Jesus ate the
Passover and then He offered Himself.

#278
The Levitical law was a means of fulfilling in flesh
what could not be fulfilled until God took on flesh:
death, resurrection and communion.

#279
In conviction of sin, Christ humbles us that we
might be blameless. In conversion, Christ declares us
blameless that we might be humbled.

#280
The resurrection of Christ took every species
of "religious diversity" and placed the Gospel
at the top of the food chain.

ASCENSION

#281
Theology which ignores biblical architecture puts
an oven in the bathroom, a toilet in the kitchen,
and builds a house on sand.

#282
Man says we need laws against fossil fuels to get
better weather. God says if we keep His Laws
He will send better weather.

#283
At the Lord's table, His flesh and blood become our bread
and wine, so we beat our swords into plowshares.

#284
Your pastor is your shepherd, not your sheepdog.

#285
Revelation begins with "Adam" and ends with
the revelation of "Eve." Thus all the bloodshed
in between occurs "in Him."

#286
The New Covenant fulfillment of the Mosaic
tithe is indeed specified: It is the saints themselves
as living sacrifices.

#287
God gave us food to teach us about life and death.
God gave us sacrifice to teach us about
death and resurrection.

BIRDS OF THE AIR

#288
God ended animal sacrifice by becoming
consumable (flesh and blood) and rising from the dead
(bread and wine).

#289
There were consumables before the Fall. That is not death.
The Fall made Adam, his offspring, and animals,
all flesh and blood, consumable.

#290
Jesus' sheep are not those who hear His voice as in
"Hear, O Israel" but those who recognize it
as the voice of their Shepherd.

#291
Jesus lifted "bridal" bread and wine out of Passover's body,
just as Firstfruits was offered during Unleavened Bread.

#292
Bread and wine is morning and evening,
light and darkness in edible form
for the judges of the earth.

#293
The Lord's Table is for dangerous people.

#294
The New Testament writers rarely use the word
"Covenant" Why? Because Christ is Himself the
New Covenant. It is not a document but a Person.

ASCENSION

#295
Most theological debates can be solved with reference
to sacred architecture. The answers are hidden
in plain sight, but nobody's looking.

#296
Dominionists just want to plant and are
suspicious of harvest. Revivalists expect a harvest every
week. Good thing Jesus holds the sickle.

#297
If you are drawn to the Table by anything (parents,
society, "Covenant,") other than the voice of Christ
by the Spirit, it's not for you.

#298
God gave Moses tablets of law we couldn't obey.
God gave Christ a scroll of inheritance we couldn't earn.

#299
The Tabernacle was built to become flesh,
pattern life, and predict the future.

#300
At the Last Passover, Jesus and the disciples ate lambs.
At the New Supper, Jesus called the disciples to be lambs.

#301
Man cannot live on economic theory alone.

BIRDS OF THE AIR

#302
The God of the Bible isn't limited to any domain.
He isn't a household god—He is a Household.

#303
Every one of God's darlings ends up on the altar.

#304
The difference between external law (stoicheia) and
internal law (Spirit) is like that between an expert
tenpin bowler and kids' guiderails.

#305
The law – intended to make life more abundant –
was used as a weapon by Satan and the Pharisees.
Do we do the same with our Confessions?

#306
Acts 10:10-12 is proof that there is bacon in heaven.

#307
Before the Last Supper, Jesus was not the New Covenant
in blood but the Old Covenant in flesh.

#308
The Ark was taken by God so there would be
no question of whether the Law was now written
on the hearts of Israel.

#309
The treasure hidden in the field is a goblet hidden in a
sack of grain, kingly dominion hidden in priestly service.

ASCENSION

#310
The Temple is to the Tabernacle as Eve is to Adam.
She takes his contents and multiplies them by ten.
And ten is a military number.

#311
Is the Lord's Supper a bittersweet scroll?

#312
Christians don't need more fads, buzz words
or slogans. What they need is men who can open
the Bible for them as a complete "world."

#313
Salvation begins with Isaac, the miraculous Son:
You shall know the truth (binding)
and the truth shall make you free (loosing).

#314
Sacramentalism allows Protestants to keep
something akin to the veneration of Mary
under the guise of the motherly Church.

#315
The problem at the heart of sacramentalism
is its failure to distinguish between hearers and speakers.
The rites are for Gospel witnesses.

#316
...in the dim corners of the chamber were strewn the
tattered remains of the books he had devoured.

BIRDS OF THE AIR

#317
Radical Christianity and radical Islam both appeal
to young men: the first to the best in them and
the latter to the worst in them.

#318
There's a reason that every single word
of the Bible, including the New Testament,
was written by men, and not women.

#319
When it comes to preaching, only a blameless,
bloodied, sacrificial lamb is worthy to open the scroll.

#320
The pen is mightier than the sword
because the Word became flesh.

#321
The New Covenant table is not about access to salvation
but about access to the throne as a legal mediator.

#322
Sermon skeletons are like the skinny cows
from the Nile – a sure sign of impending famine.

#323
Sacrificing a blameless substitute on an unhewn altar
turned hearts of stone into a heart of flesh.

#324
True sheep don't complain about being shepherded.

ASCENSION

#325
All God's Covenants are conditional, but the
New Covenant is conditional on the obedience of Christ.

#326
Meekness is a willingness to be pliable under
godly authority and an unwillingness to be pliable
under ungodly authority.

#327
Fathers, your job is to keep everyone else's tank full,
so you'd better be a refinery.

#328
Joseph's obedience led to the distribution of grain.
Daniel's led to the scattering of Israel
and the distribution of the Word.

#329
"Seeking first" the kingdom means
submitting like a priest.

#330
Baptism by immersion is humiliating.
And that is the point.
It is a sign of humility before God and His Church.

#331
"How-to" books on transformation sidestep the
inconvenient, uncomfortable and unpopular truth:
put the flesh on the altar and keep it there.

BIRDS OF THE AIR

#332
For the "Firstfruits" nation of Israel, circumcision was a pruning, not actual fruit. This was the mistake of the unbelieving Jews.

#333
BAPTIST PREACHERS ALWAYS SEEM TO HAVE CAPS LOCK ON WHEN THEY WRITE SERMONS.

#334
By the Spirit, the saints gathered the Canon. By the Spirit, the Canon gathered the saints. The sheep know the Shepherd's voice.

#335
Many westerners anxiously strip the bloody flesh from their menus precisely because we Christians have stripped it from our religion.

#336
If the offerings, burnt whole, turned into dust and smoke a substitute for Adam, what did it mean when the new Mosaic priesthood ate them?

#337
The eschatological feast is the one where the intimacy of marriage is actually between every member of the body and thus not in this life.

#338
Godly conversations around the dinner table with your kids end up toppling godless empires.

ASCENSION

#339
The economic state of every nation is evidence of the rule of the ascended Christ and His administration of Covenant blessings and curses.

#340
The New Covenant: Christ on your lips, aid in your hands, and the world at your feet.

#341
We eat Jesus' flesh and drink His blood because we are a valley of dry ... ribs.

#342
Animals can survive on food alone. Men also require a steady diet of truth.

#343
Acknowledging God in everything we do costs us little but brings Him great pleasure.

#344
The good things in life were not meant to be used to mask the underlying despair of your mortality, but to awaken in you a gratitude to God.

#345
God rips Christian men open to build a safe place for others. So, when suffering, identify with the dead lion and praise God for the honey.

BIRDS OF THE AIR

#346
The Old Testament is a violent, bloody book,
but the more we modern Christians neglect it,
the more our Gospel loses its teeth.

#347
The God of the Old Testament is a butcher only
because the Christ of the New Testament is a chef.

#348
The Bible is a priestly Tree of Life.
If we submit to it, it becomes a Kingly Tree of Wisdom.
Disobedience brings stupidity.

#349
Genesis 3 cursed Land and womb. Sarai received the
fertility of the plain, and the cities receive the "salty"
barrenness of her womb.

#350
Humble yourself before God in the morning and He
won't need to humble you as much through the day.

#351
The Bible teaches us not to bow to idols,
but instead to bow to each other, as images of God.

#352
If our churches were actually hungry and thirsty for
righteousness, they would come to the Table every week.

ASCENSION

#353
We taste God personally, but
we only feast on Him corporately.

#354
Preterists celebrate the Lord's Supper because
AD70 was not the culmination of the
New Covenant era but the inauguration.

#355
A sermon should give a man a fish
AND teach him how to fish.

#356
Israel lived permanently at the gate of God
bearing offerings. Consequently, his is a
long history of Cains and Abels.

#357
When Jesus told Peter to feed His sheep, they both
knew those sheep were heading for the altar.

#358
We regard the detailed architectural descriptions in the
Bible as antiquated oddities instead of diagrammatical
expositions of the Trinity.

#359
Perhaps our food allergies, dietary obsessions
and eating disorders simply result from our failure
to ask God's blessing as we receive.

BIRDS OF THE AIR

#360
Molech was simply another dragon hijacking the offspring of the woman with an offer of certain food.

#361
God's commitment to Abraham meant a history of resurrections for an Israel continually bent on death. Mt. Moriah sealed that promise.

#362
The socialist, the secularist and the satanist love nothing more than Ethics divorced from Covenant with God.

#363
Contrary to popular teaching, the Bible does not condescend to man at all. God does not talk down to us. He calls us up.

#364
If the role of "government minister" included the MP* interceding before God for his/her portfolio, we would see real progress.

#365
The world can only be reconstructed with guidance from a holy man with a vision from God.

#366
The Law wasn't given to bring life. It was given to expose the fakes so we would seek the Life.

---

*Member of Parliament.

ASCENSION

#367
As Israel, Jesus is all the tribes.
As Levi, He is the firstfruits;
as Judah, kingly succession, etc.

#368
God cursed the ground and the womb. Ruth begins with famine and childlessness. The curse is removed through the marriage of Jew and Gentile.

#369
Yahweh wasn't like a pagan god, limited to one territory or high place. He moved from mountain to mountain, just like Jacob set up stones.

#370
Communion takes a body of sin which was fully grown and serves it to us as a source of new life.

#371
Gender is a Covenantal office delegated by God.

#372
Attract monkeys with peanuts.
Attract vultures with carrion.
Attract groupies with rockstars.
Attract sheep with the Shepherd.

#373
It could be said that the Church is the ultimate pyramid scheme but it's actually a ziggurat.

BIRDS OF THE AIR

#374
The Firstfruits Church (AD30-70) was the "devoted" spoil of Jeshua's first conquest.

#375
Every week, the past is broken like flesh and poured out like blood. Then it's given back to us as the future, as bread and wine.

#376
In parenting, in farming, in discipleship, we plant with an expectation, not a guarantee, of an increase.

#377
In the 4th century, as in the 1st, a single copy of the New Testament required the death of an entire flock of sheep.

#378
Oil is liquid light. The darkness flees.
Water is liquid healing. The flow of blood stops.

#379
God gave us many chapters of sacred architecture to illustrate the nature of the Trinity and how it shapes the world. We skip over them.

#380
It was Esau's selling of his birthright which led to his losing the Covenant succession. The Edomite Herods attempted to steal it all back.

ASCENSION

#381
God's kitchen has recipes for seeds, vegetables and meat right up to human sacrifice, which requires a lot of bench space and preparation.

#382
The most effective but neglected "frontline" of evangelism in your church might be simple hospitality.

#383
Biblical architecture, however obscure, is the most profound and potent form of "promise."

#384
The fact that the Land promises culminated in a "heavenly country" should not surprise us. That's what the Levites always had.

#385
The Church should be curing biblical illiteracy, not pandering to it.

#386
Why is it that those who occupy themselves with the Law of God are so often the ones who are merciless with men?

#387
While theologians speak of salvation in merely legal terms, the Word of God never speaks of it outside of legal-sacrificial terms.

BIRDS OF THE AIR

#388
If your church only has Communion four times a year,
Jesus is outside knocking on the door most Sundays.

#389
The OT is mystifying without an understanding of
Covenant. The New is mystifying without the
understanding that Jesus IS the Covenant.

#390
As my grandfather said, "The trials of life will make you
bitter or better." Either way, you are food.

#391
Jesus was slain at the Place of the Skull
because the Head was offered first in Leviticus 1.
And Peter was to feed the Body for slaughter.

#392
The depths of the Incarnation can only be
understood in the context of Levitical Law.

#393
Because the Jewish rulers and their followers
would not be bread for the nations,
Jesus made them the meat on the table.

#394
Western masculinity exalted itself.
Western masculinity is being humbled.

ASCENSION

#395
For Christ, bread and wine were a deforming (flesh) and an emptying out (blood). For us they are a new Creation, a forming and a filling.

#396
When Jesus said, "I have food to eat that you do not know about," He was not talking about a private stash of sacramental bread and wine.

#397
Since the dead are raised, let us eat and drink with Jesus, for tomorrow we die.

#398
Communion is the firstfruits of the land (bread and wine) and the womb (flesh and blood) given to us as the firstborn from the dead.

#399
Adolescence is when one pushes boundaries, thinks one knows everything, and rejects the wisdom of elders. That's where the Church is now.

#400
By representing kingly Esau as a priestly man, Jacob saved him from judgment.

#401
A book on the Trinity with no reference to sacred architecture is like the lack of a simile in the latter half of this sentence.

BIRDS OF THE AIR

#402
Sacred architecture is "measured out" in
human flesh in narrative. Ignore this and our exegesis
is fumbling around in a darkened room.

#403
Biblical scholarship is essential, like maintaining
a serviceable pantry. But let's not pretend that it
contains anything edible.

#404
Children were included in the worship in Exodus 24
but excluded from the sanctuary meal.
How inconvenient. Let's ignore that, shall we?

#405
Warhol's art was all about food, sex and death.
Like Leviticus.

#406
The disciples didn't "meet Jesus in the sacraments."

#407
Because the flesh of Christ is in heaven,
the Spirit can be sent to earth.

#408
Moses received engraved stones to thresh the heirs.
Jesus received an inheritance scroll of parchment:
law written on flesh.

ASCENSION

#409
When we fast, we become broken bread
and poured out wine.

#410
An Aaronic priest could not drink wine in the
presence of God. Thus, a man or woman under the
Nazirite vow was always in the presence of God.

#411
The altar devours Adam as dust and ashes,
swallowed by the earth like the sons of Korah.
But the fire also creates fragrant bridal smoke.

#412
Firstfruits: Our unwillingness to give God anything is tied
to our rejection of the idea that we wither as grass.

#413
Cain and Abel brought offerings "at the end of days."
It makes sense that Abel was avenged in "the last days,"
the ascension of firstfruits.

#414
Jesus' bread behaves like leaven. It multiplies!
He turns the end into a new beginning.

#415
Foxes have holes (Moses), and birds of the air have nests
(Elijah), but the Son of Man, as true Levite, ministers
between heaven and earth.

BIRDS OF THE AIR

#416
God calls us to be lambs (priests) that He might make us lions (kings). Men who style themselves as lions inevitably become wolves.

#417
Moses was not merely a hearer but a humble hearer and thus a mighty doer.

#418
Risk is a qualifier of great culture as it is of great men.

#419
A Vegan meal is like a sentence made of adjectives without any nouns.

#420
Both the believing and unbelieving Jews were ground to powder – the first as fine flour and the second as a golden calf.

#421
Those who reject the need for a priesthood unwittingly and inevitably set up their own.

#422
For the legalist, sacrifice is not substitutionary but an offering of his own flesh.

#423
Systematic theology is a means of identifying ingredients that renders the meal inedible.

ASCENSION

#424
Apparently, sacred architecture was not
given for our edification.

#425
Males are not natures to be tamed
but arrows to be aimed.

#426
Cherubim have four wings because they are
related to the earth. They are the sacrificial sword
and the four cornered altar.

#427
A vision from God will always be costly
because a vision from God is a blueprint
for a building on a site that is already occupied.

#428
The Tabernacle was an Adamic dwelling covered
in skins. This was removed and its innards were
incorporated into a Bridal Temple.

#429
At the hands of men, Jesus wore a crown of thorns.
At the hand of the Father, Jesus wore a crown of horns.

#430
If child's play is "life training without consequences,"
what are adult gamers training for?

BIRDS OF THE AIR

#431
The world doesn't care about the
Lord's Table until it leaves the building
on the legs and in the mouths of His prophets.

#432
We must not be so heavenly-minded that we retreat
from the world nor so earthly-minded that
we are disqualified from God's blessing.

#433
My theological thinking might seem
rigid and inflexible, but this is because
its blueprint is sacred architecture.

#434
The Confessions are not a metal band
around the Tree but a growth ring,
preventing a return to old errors
yet allowing God to speak anew.

> "*Christian ethics is an ethics of the Spirit.
> This is enough to separate it
> from every other ethics.*"
>
> — Edward Tingley

TESTING

#435
An angel of light from heaven,
or a false prophet on earth,
will always tell you exactly
what you want to hear.

#436
Islam revels in the sword because
it has no spiritual weapons.

#437
Once it was Jews (priests) and Romans (kings) against the Church (prophets). Now it's Islam and Secularism. We already know how this ends.

#438
The idea that Jesus watches us through the eyes of the poor comes from bad exegesis. The homeless are not God's CCTV.

#439
Sometimes a word in season is salt.
Sometimes it is a flogging, and then salt.

#440
The darkness upon Jerusalem at noonday was the same darkness which covered Egypt and Pharaoh's armies... the dark side of the glory cloud.

BIRDS OF THE AIR

#441
Separating giver from gifts began in Eden.
Kick out the Church (personal generosity),
and the State (impersonal entitlement) fills the void.

#442
New Covenant theonomy is Pentecostal.
It is "internal law," the Spirit dwelling in the repentant,
obedient believer, a lamp in every temple.

#443
Religious, political and economic ideologies
are a symptom of Adam's willingness
to identify evil anywhere but in himself.

#444
Forming and filling, duty and pleasure,
suffering and glory, Stoicism and Hedonism,
are twin beats in one heart.

#445
In the flesh we obey out of fear. In the Spirit we obey
out of love. Perfect (mature) love casts out fear.

#446
Since Pentecost, the fire of God's love can purify.
The saints ascend as fragrant smoke.
The sinners fall into the altar as ashes and dust.

TESTING

#447
Given the choice between Christ and Barabbas, or Christ and Mohammed, the crowd will always choose the murderer.

#448
When Peter said "You and your children," he was speaking to the circumcised who swore, "Let His blood be upon us and upon our children."

#449
Jeroboam rid Israel of Levitical priests, so God sent prophets. The background for this is the death of Abel and the witness of his blood.

#450
God sent angels to Sodom as legal witnesses, and fire fell from heaven. That fire is now in us as the brimstone witnesses. (2 Cor. 2:16)

#451
John the Baptist lost his head for challenging Herod on adultery. Perhaps John should have focused on helping the poor.

#452
If you have to redefine everything sacred to protect a cherished practice, chances are that practice is grievous error.

BIRDS OF THE AIR

#453
The problem with writing your own narrative about a situation is that you most often end up believing it.

#454
We are not only bone of His bones,
and flesh of His flesh,
but also Spirit of His Spirit.

#455
Sin is either an attempted manipulation of God
or a selfish manipulation of the world.

#456
If I were a politician and got called out for something I tweeted, I would find a clever way to blame it on auto spellcheck.

#457
The cross was victory disguised as defeat.
Immoral legislation is defeat disguised as victory.

#458
Christians argue about the right thing to do in complicated situations, as though it can be "legislated." The apostles relied on the Spirit.

#459
Jesus tells us we should pluck out an eye.
Samson and Zedekiah tell us we will see better.

TESTING

#460
The cure for darkness isn't found
in a detailed study of darkness.

#461
Just as the perfect Law reveals our unrighteousness,
so does the blamelessness of Christ.

#462
We don't find in the Bible the kind of sentimentality
which plagues the Western Church because persecution
calls us beyond mere sentiment.

#463
The fact that the Church is conscious of its failings
is the work of the Spirit and a promise of glory.
Paganism is always "perfect."

#464
What is the Great Tree? If we put kingdom first,
being food and shelter for others,
God will feed and cover us (Matt. 6:33; 1 Tim. 6:8).

#465
Jesus posted and tweeted challenging stuff until
everyone unfollowed and unliked Him.

#466
Sin is passionate, but obedience is not dispassionate.
It is a willingness to delay our gratification
until God's time.

BIRDS OF THE AIR

#467
Is regeneration an event or a process?
Well, a family dinner is a process, but there is a point
at which the raw food becomes acceptable.

#468
God will not be tested on our terms (Matthew 4:7),
but He calls every man to test Him,
through obedience, on His (Matthew 16:25).

#469
The death of the West, as with the demise
of all great civilizations, will be an inside job.

#470
The sexual act follows the Covenant pattern.
We must ask what sex says about the Covenant,
and what the Covenant says about sex.

#471
The first Social Justice Warriors were the men
who brought to Jesus the woman caught in adultery.

#472
Trusting any theological school or tradition to
interpret the Scriptures for you without question
is not understanding but laziness.

#473
Why do so few perceive the state's Messianic
pretensions in its claim to control the weather
through an increase in taxation?

TESTING

#474
You'd comprehend the Bible better if you
stopped reading and just looked at the pictures.

#475
If your pastor teaches that the Church now has
the Bible under its belt and needs to look elsewhere
for wisdom, you need to go elsewhere.

#476
For assurance and encouragement, we turn to
tomes of pietism and biography. But God gave us
discomforting songs and pages of architecture.

#477
So, let me get this straight: the incarnation of Christ
is the reason that venerating icons is okay,
not the very reason to reject them?

#478
The Church suffers a very modern breed of illiterate,
an educated elite deliberately un-schooled
of native literary instinct.

#479
We don't break God's laws so much as bounce off them.

#480
God cannot be separated from either His
attributes or His gifts. To have a God-given
internal moral compass is to have God Himself.

BIRDS OF THE AIR

#481
The Apostles turned the world upside down because it was time for the second half of the chiasm.

#482
The seven churches up in Asia are a constellation, a new "Lampstand" overlooking the "Table" of Jerusalem, soon to be a "Firstfruits" bloodbath.

#483
Joseph didn't know Mary until after Christ was born – because the threshing floor has to wait until after Firstfruits.

#484
The Old Testament might be the basement, but it's most definitely Top Shelf.

#485
Open Theists might have open minds, but they have closed Bibles.

#486
The Law made the Judaizers proud instead of humble. Jesus' cup makes you bold as a drunkard (Acts 2:13).

#487
Since the Bible is a mosaic, a weave as tight as Leviathan's scales, why is so much theology a collection of disconnected little boxes?

TESTING

#488
The Bible's matrix means that every part of the Bible is a commentary on every other part of the Bible.

#489
The sermon should be fruit from a living branch, not an assemblage of artificial evergreen twigs with candies attached.

#490
Celebrate your tradition if it upholds the Scriptures. But don't make excuses for it where it overrides them.

#491
Defending a theological tradition is like following a football team. One is tempted to explain away its fumbles, foibles, errors and losses.

#492
Pet doctrines and practices that need to be protected from the Bible and supported by tradition are idols that we love more than the truth.

#493
If that chiasm you think you see doesn't really go anywhere and returns "void," it may not be the Word of the Lord.

#494
Roman Catholic theologians are well worth reading, but it's pizza with anchovies – always a chance of swallowing something fishy.

BIRDS OF THE AIR

#495
He who exults in Augustine, Calvin and Barth but never
rejoices in the Bible is a fanboy, not a theologian.

#496
Ignore the theologian who tells you "It can't mean that!"
but then can't tell you what it actually means.

#497
Fear of heresy has become fear of the text.

#498
We hanker for the next "life-changing book"
because we are so disconnected from the Bible.

#499
Seminary students fed on straw
cannot produce the weekly golden egg.

#500
"Strange" fire and "stranger" are uses of the same
Hebrew word. What the sons of Aaron did
in Leviticus 10, all Israel did in Numbers 25.

#501
Europe is helpless against Islam because fire must be
fought with fire, and the Spirit has departed.

#502
The problem with Islamic "sojourners" is Islam.
Islam brings both the stranger and the strange fire.

TESTING

#503
It strikes me that the Bible simply isn't interested in most of the issues with which theologians habitually occupy themselves.

#504
The Law was an app. The Spirit is an OS.

#505
Don't wait for power to be holy. Just do it. Holiness is empowering. That's how it's supposed to work.

#506
The reason we abandon Church is often the very reason the Lord wants us there: the challenge of loving.

#507
Regarding John Piper's Christian Hedonism, I think I've got the Hedonism bit under my belt. Still working on the Christian bit.

#508
The R2K debate is a pointless dispute over legal jurisdiction, that is, law, when the kingdom of God is a jurisdiction of Spirit.*

#509
Our God spoke the Word and turned temptation into power, suffering into a weapon, and death into victory.

---

*R2K is an abbreviation which refers to the debate over Reformed "two kingdoms" theology. Asserting that the concept of "two kingdoms" relates to Church and State rather than "heaven and earth" or "spirit and body" erroneously limits the "legal" moral authority of the Gospel to those within the Church.

BIRDS OF THE AIR

#510
Nebuchadnezzar's Gospel: a proud Lion humbled
to eat grass like an Ox, with Eagle's feathers,
who finally became a faithful Man.

#511
Internal law is the gift of the seer,
the presence of the One from whose eyes
nothing in heaven or on earth is hidden.

#512
Our greatest strengths are nearly always
the flip side of our greatest weaknesses.

#513
If you want to speak the truth, drink spirits.
If you want to speak the truth in love, drink the Spirit.

#514
The Philistines were a highly cultured branch of
Egyptian civilization. Goliath wasn't all brawn.

#515
Architecturally, David was the bronze altar (man of blood)
and Solomon the golden altar (inside the house –
the only bloodshed a memorial).

#516
The cold, calculating and heartless have an advantage:
Immune to warm, sentimental trappings,
they often see the logical heart of a matter.

TESTING

#517
The only reason that the Church is still around
is because God is in it.

#518
Satan is hopeless at typology, which is why
he always gets tenure in the academies.

#519
Doctor Jesus' X-rays can be a midlife crisis
or a call to martyrdom.

#520
The darkness only lasts until God's will is done.
Then the Veil is torn away.

#521
Christ was "the voice from the midst of the darkness"
on Sinai – and again on Golgotha.

#522
The Tents and Temples were all crosses laid out
on the ground. But the cross was the first tent
lifted upright once filled with God.

#523
There's a gut-wrenching irony in a
carpenter nailed to a hewn tree.

#524
There is only one thing worse than never hearing
the Gospel: hearing it and rejecting it.

BIRDS OF THE AIR

#525
Jesus was crucified with robbers because Adam was a thief. Like Cain and Abel, one blasphemed and the other joined Him in Paradise.

#526
Aaronic priests were bloodied on the right side: ear, hand and foot. Jesus was bloodied on both, "to make in himself of twain one new man."

#527
The confused contradictions of the left (pro-gay, pro-Islam, pro-women, pro-choice) are the spawn of a single anti-Christian hatred.

#528
Was Jesus a Calvinist or an Arminian? Both. The incarnation was the sovereignty of God and the will of Man united at last.

#529
God always uses the tyranny of a Saul to prepare a David for rule.

#530
The blessing for obedience to the Covenant was dominion over the beasts... The Covenant curse, however, was to be eaten by them.

#531
The expectations of God always trump the expectations of men, even godly ones.

TESTING

#532
In Revelation 2-3, Jesus trims the wicks of the
lampstand churches that Babylon (Jerusalem)
might be judged in their light (Daniel 5:5).

#533
Jesus desires His new people to be hot and cold,
fire and water, coming out of Egypt.

#534
Jeremiah's call to submit to Babylon
and the woman's anointing of Jesus for death
both heralded the birth of a new kind of Israel.

#535
Solomon's great white throne pictured the Lord's:
He first tries the hearts that He might then
judge the souls (1 Kings 3:16-28).

#536
When a Christian turns back from
following Jesus, Satan has found his "price."
It is redemption in reverse.

#537
"Sure, we disagree, but let's aim for peace.
Let's be grown up about this. Let's dialogue." – Satan

#538
Jesus' use of "sheep without a shepherd"
is not only another swipe at the Herods, it is a
reference to Jerusalem as new Babylon (Is. 13:14).

BIRDS OF THE AIR

#539
Reading the Scriptures "in the light of" any
uninspired literature is too often the resort of those
who refuse to read them typologically.

#540
When sin gets you down, remember that
Peter denied Christ and Paul killed Christians.
Our Master welcomes the contrite and loves to forgive.

#541
Gifted Christians must submit to Church authority,
but so often it is the fearful "spirit of Admin"
which quenches the work of the Spirit.

#542
I hate the Bible. Reading it puts my selfish nature to death.
I love the Bible. I always come away from it renewed.

#543
Mastery of the Bible comes only after solitude,
wrestling till dawn, a permanent wound,
and insistence on a blessing.

#544
What do you do when a student writes the Ten
Commandments on his arm to cheat in a Bible class test?

#545
Jacob realized that every serpentine challenge
came from the hand of God. He crushed them through
crafty obedience and gained great wisdom.

TESTING

#546
The opposite of a life of faith is not a life of doubt
but a life of fear.

#547
We will take risks for pleasure,
and often the heart of the pleasure is the risk.
But will we take risks for the kingdom?

#548
It's time the menora became a Christian symbol.
Why is it used by those who rejected,
and still reject, Pentecost?

#549
Both Yahweh and Satan desire to open our eyes.
Both call us to "taste and see."
But only Yahweh tastes good.

#550
The human frame was designed to thrive
only under difficulty. Ask any body builder.

#551
Thankfully, the redemption of the Christian's mind
is gradual. We squint at every new judicial revelation,
but God spares the retinas.

#552
Is it reformation we need, or revival?
The first is putting cut meat on the altar;
the second setting it on fire. Each alone is useless.

BIRDS OF THE AIR

#553
Only dull or lazy minds are content to ignore
the mysterious parts of the Bible.

#554
Modern historians take advantage of biblical illiteracy
to present dumb, dishonest and easily-dismissed ideas.

#555
The Words from God were not enough.
To actually build the Tabernacle,
Bezalel and Aholiab also needed the Spirit.

#556
If we weren't so self-deluded about our cravenness and
mortality, we'd see how exciting the Gospel really is.

#557
So, pastor, explaining a Gospel text with a Torah type
is eisegesis, but using a baseball anecdote is OK?
Can I hit you out of the park?

#558
Hindrances and disabilities all come with
corresponding gifts of which the finest and
most precious is humility.

#559
If your Church has 12 major doctrines and one of
them causes major problems in the other 11,
chances are that that one doctrine is an idol.

TESTING

#560
Systematic theology is like listening to a symphony
to count how many times a B flat is played.

#561
We are at our best when we are undone.

#562
Our culture's "remedy" for the failure of a man
to lay down his freedom for a woman is a woman's
refusal to lay down her freedom for a child.

#563
Zombie Christians, wandering aimlessly in the flesh,
the living dead not the dead living, unable to speak,
digesting other people's brains.

#564
Like yeast, the kingdom of light grows better in the dark.

#565
We cannot command him to whom we are
still bowing for counterfeit kingdom.

#566
What are the Gospels? Four bloodied altar horns
waiting for the holy fire of Pentecost.

#567
Those who consult the Reformers before they consult
Moses and the Prophets to make sense of the New
Testament are replicating Talmudism.

BIRDS OF THE AIR

#568
Even the most mundane chore is the history
of the world hidden in a riddle.

#569
It's not that Jesus doesn't crack any jokes
in the Gospels. It's that we don't know Moses
and the Prophets well enough to get them.

#570
There are three Babylons in Bible history.
The first was priestly, the second was kingly,
and the last was prophetic.

#571
I've learned that the reason most theologians
don't deal with the Text is not because it is unsophisticated
but because the theologians are.

#572
God likes stories, but that means that He also likes
suspense and drama, intrigue and provocativeness.
Look at the Book He gave us!

#573
Too many well-read Christians know the
Reformers and Puritans far better than they know
their Bibles. Too lazy to chew for yourself?

#574
How you feel about Jesus is directly related
to how you feel about your own sin.

TESTING

#575
By faith, hungry thieves like Adam are
filled with good things and become
food and shelter for others. (Ephesians 4:28)

#576
Aaron's two sons were unworthy and consumed,
but the Babylonian fire glorified the three Jews
and made them an acceptable offering.

#577
God sends darkness and confusion among
His enemies to make them self-destructive.
This includes sexual confusion.

#578
If you aren't letting the Lord breathe into your ministry,
the best it can ever be is a man-shaped pile of dust.

#579
The Bible doesn't take sides on predestination.
It simply says that the Gospel is a fire and men are
either fragrant smoke or dusty ashes.

#580
Some Christians are slow to accept new ideas
from the Bible. But other Christians are just slow.

#581
It amazes me how much time pastors and theologians
can spend talking about the Bible without
ever actually dealing with the text.

BIRDS OF THE AIR

#582
The Bible's accumulation of objects,
people and events means that by the time the reader
gets to Revelation, every word is a hyperlink.

#583
The Bible recasts the shape of the way we think
in order to forge the shape of the way we live.

#584
An Adam governed by God's Law
is an Adam fit to govern.

#585
Covenant is a choice between God's device
and the gods of our own devising.

#586
Imagine if Bible teachers learned that God gave us
Tolkien, Lewis and even Rowling as gateway drugs
to the Scriptures for moderns.

#587
Being discipled by a conservative modernist is like
getting a skateboard with three wheels for Christmas.

#588
A saint and a sinner have the same Adamic heart, but by
the Spirit of God, the saint is as appalled by it as God is.

#589
Not only is God just, but His justice is poetic.

TESTING

#590
The blind Pharisees' sin was pitting the Scriptures against Jesus. Our own blindness often pits Jesus against the Scriptures. They are one.

#591
If I were tempted in the wilderness, Satan would offer to lock me up for 20 years, with a single window, a bed, my books and a computer.

#592
Judah's three sons were named Watchman, Strength and Prosperity. Not one of them did what it said on the tin.

#593
Adversity is supposed to make your heart softer, not harder. Just in case you find yourself at a crossroads any time soon.

#594
Why is it OK to be excited about any book except the Bible? It runs rings around anything else for plot, beauty and complexity.

#595
In Romans 1, God gives up those who reject Him three times. In Philippians 2, Jesus gives Himself up three times.

#596
If I see one more non-biblical Holy Week analogy I'm going to deck somebody. With the Old Testament.

BIRDS OF THE AIR

#597
If you use the word *kenosis* in an English sentence,
you are either lazy or pretentious.

#598
Dogs and pigs are scavengers. They represent the
Church and the State "on the take."

#599
It's wrong to impose a system on the Scriptures
where they are fuzzy, but it's wrong to revel in fuzziness
when Scripture presents a system.

#600
Reading and teaching the Bible without an eidetic
mindset is viewing and sharing God's digital
photos as computer code.

#601
The house of God stands only because God Himself
dwells within. When He departs, the godless vacuum
summons the scavenging hordes.

#602
The "Pentecostal" gifts we see today are mostly
manufactured – like the limited signs of Jannes and
Jambres who withstood Moses.

#603
Generous love is the butter,
but the Gospel must remain a knife.

TESTING

#604
The Church is what happens when people glory
in the Bible and its Christ. Apostasy is what happens
when people glory in the Church.

#605
Heaven came down and glory incinerated the sacrifice.
And the priests of Baal were slaughtered and washed away.

#606
The Lord withdrew His Spirit from Saul,
then sent His Spirit in David to comfort Saul.

#607
If Jesus is Lord, what do we do with Caesar?
Be faithful and wait for the Lord to send Constantine.

#608
Adam's obedience would have opened the Land to him,
and also opened the womb. The curse on Land
and womb was in fact a limited blessing.

#609
Every temptation is a call to sacrifice the future
on the altar of now. In many cases,
this involves offspring, as it did for Adam.

#610
Jewish "apocalyptic" mimicked the prophets
for the same reason the book of Mormon mimicked
the KJV: to sound authoritative.

BIRDS OF THE AIR

#611
Murderers and adulterers were put to death
in Israel because murder and adultery
would be put to death in Christ.

#612
Proof texting from the Bible is like retrieving
the three eggs out of the cake you baked.

#613
Why is rebellion as the sin of divination?
Rebels want the miraculous increase promised by God
without meeting His conditions. (Rev 13:13)

#614
When the book of Leviticus is music to your ears,
you are comprehending the Spirit of the Law.

#615
How many Christians turn up to Church
every week hungry for steak and are offered a nipple?
Pastors, it's time to wean your people.

#616
Revelation was not written in code to avoid persecution.
Ezekiel uses the same language. Its sacred images
were a call to avoid judgment.

#617
Elisha didn't have a problem with peak oil.
He knew God would provide, and that shiny oil is a
kingly blessing to be used in faith.

TESTING

#618
How far is going too far with your girlfriend or fiancée?
Until the wedding, in God's eyes, she's your sister.

#619
The entire Word of God is poetry and song,
yet we have a generation of Bible teachers
without a poetic or musical bone in their bodies.

#620
Relishing the minutiae of holy laws is foreign to the
holistic Spirit of those laws who delights in purity.

#621
There is no liberty (or libertarianism) without the
Spirit of the Lord (2 Cor 3:17). Freedom from the
Church is always bondage to the State.

#622
In the wilderness, Jesus refused a satanic offer
of the kingdoms of the world. Satan left him –
and offered it to the Herods.

#623
Relying on word studies to make sense of Scripture is like
relying on color studies to make sense of a painting.

#624
The darkness of the human mind is the reason
scholars insist that the Bible must bow before
ancient pagan literature at every turn.

BIRDS OF THE AIR

#625
In any debate, especially theological ones, tradition,
rank and consensus can support an argument
but are no substitute for it.

#626
Making generalizations, however true,
about the purpose of the Old Testament, without dealing
with its obvious weirdness, is a cop-out.

#627
I've been reading the Bible for over 35 years,
and I'm still finding Easter eggs.

#628
The Bible is the most beautiful thing I have ever seen.

#629
The Bible is a woven cloth. There are no
hermeneutical rules. There are living connections.

#630
The Bible is written in "slit scan," a linear recording of
exactly the same location over a period of time.

#631
Knees bowed to Jesus are royal knees.

#632
As mediators between heaven and earth,
each of us is to be a tiny, holy flame
purifying its own earthy body.

TESTING

#633
Our attempts to contain, control or direct
the work of the Spirit are like dry leaves
ganging up on the wind.

#634
When the Spirit is quenched, God departs slowly.
But when He is obeyed, He returns
like a mighty, rushing wind.

#635
The prophets provoked the sons of Jacob to jealousy
just as Jacob provoked the sons of Leah.

#636
The Left might be godless, but
the Right has only the form of godliness.

#637
Perhaps the most surprising biblical teaching
is that lawlessness begins with breaking the law of God
and ends with tyranny via legislation.

#638
Jesus said "Without me you can do nothing,"
because they, like the Herods, thought they
could do it by Covenant.

#639
Biblical leprosy is scaled (serpentine) skin.
Paul's conversion removed the scales from his
draconian eyes and he stopped breathing fire.

BIRDS OF THE AIR

#640
Is it futile to look for one's own theological blind spot?

#641
When the Bible Matrix is your hammer,
everything actually IS a nail.

#642
It is ironic that the Holy Grail of biblical theology –
the Covenant key – is the very concept of quest.

#643
The Bible isn't written in chapters or verses.
It is written in festal harvest cycles.

#644
Make arbitrary connections between Scriptures
and nobody bats an eyelid. Track the actual
poetic structure and everyone loses their minds.

#645
Investiture comes after some sort of ethical testing.
It vindicates the obedient by putting them into government.

#646
I'd rather hang out with a premillennialist who lives in
the Bible than a postmillennialist who doesn't.

#647
The Bible is more exciting and intriguing than
any movie. Christian academics are the reason why
Christians prefer movies to the Bible.

TESTING

#648
Adam's sin, as a gifted young man,
was believing that he wasn't expendable.

#649
The purpose of the law is to restrain evil not enable it.

#650
The name of the Hebrew judge
who lost his eyes means "Sunrise."

#651
In Mark 6:7, Jesus ties the disciples together in pairs,
sets them on fire and releases them into Herod's fields.

#652
Deuteronomy 17:18 states that Israel's king,
once enthroned, was to copy out the Law by hand.
Jesus is doing that in us by the Spirit.

#653
"Tolerance" in the Garden leads to murder
in the Land and annihilation in the World.

#654
Neither Israel's shoes nor the clothes of
Daniel's friends were consumed as they
"walked in the fire" with the Son of God.

#655
The times you least feel like obeying God
are the times you most need to obey Him.

BIRDS OF THE AIR

#656
The days you least feel like being in Church
are the days you most need to be there.

#657
If we want the Spirit to work,
we must first prepare a straight path for Him.
(Isa. 40:3; Mal. 3:1; Matt. 3:3; 11:10)

#658
God uses false doctrine to purify the Church.
That started in Genesis 3.

#659
I suspect that the flaws and trials peculiar to each of us
are intimately connected with the different roles
we will each fill in eternity.

#660
The work of understanding the Bible is too great
for a single mind, yet, by the Spirit, all men
will be of a single mind.

#661
God doesn't deal in facts in the way theologians do.
He deals in facts as processes, in exactly the way
theologians don't, won't or can't.

#662
I'm not worthy to untie the shoelaces of my
theological betters. But it's my duty to point out
where they've tied them together.

TESTING

#663
Preaching a Jesus separated from the rest of the Bible
is preaching another Jesus.

#664
Revelation is about the enthronement of Greater Solomon.
His first decrees wiped out His Father's enemies
and installed a new government.

#665
When Rev. 6:15 speaks of "the kings of the Land"
we are supposed to think of men like Jeroboam,
Ahab, Manasseh and Omri – that is, Herods.

#666
Satan pretends to rule heaven that he might
offer a false dominion on the earth. Thus,
all tyrants consider themselves divine.

#667
The seven bowls in Revelation came from the Lampstand
(Ex 25:31). They were the curses of the Law of Moses.

#668
The cherubim were two legal witnesses flanking
the sword, a tongue of fire. As eyes and mouth they were
the fiery face of God against Man.

#669
Just as Moses was "eye and tooth"
so Elijah was "vision and prophecy."

BIRDS OF THE AIR

#670
"It's time we left the dark ages behind,"
said a progressive, in the dark.

#671
The secularist's "advocacy" is not self-sacrifice
to uphold the law of God, but special interest lobbying
to evade or change the law of God.

#672
A spiritual vacuum cannot remain so forever.

#673
Community, relationship, and parenting are clinical,
objective words. Those who need to use the words
don't have the things they describe.

#674
Jesus' sheep hear His voice. It calls them to the altar,
and the fire transforms them into lions.

#675
Gnashing of teeth: Contemplating the use of my sleep
bruxism toothguard during the day. Is that a bad sign?

#676
The enormous Christian book industry proves
that there is no money in good theology.

#677
An academic divides the text like an expert overspecializes.
He ends up knowing everything about nothing.

TESTING

#678
"Doing what is right in your own eyes" is not necessarily lawlessness. Sometimes it's shortsightedness.

#679
The command to turn the other cheek isn't pacifism.
It's a call to the striker to either repent
or fill up his sins and be struck by God.

#680
An unwillingness to receive the Spirit of the Law
stems from a desire to use it as an instrument of death
rather than more abundant life.

#681
The Bible mediates the apostolic word to men.
Sadly, we moderns now rely on Christian fiction,
good and bad, to mediate the Bible to us.

#682
The world is constructed typologically, so poetry
is not imposed upon it but inherent in its very nature.
Naturalism is blind to nature.

#683
"Possessing our enemies' gates" today means in part the
need for Christians to choose law as a vocation.
The seat of Moses belongs to Jesus.

#684
The Son was forsaken by the Father
that we might never be forsaken by the Son.

BIRDS OF THE AIR

#685
Attempting to quantify the Spirit's work by analyzing what and whom He moves is like quantifying the wind by analyzing Autumn leaves.

#686
God laughs at the rulers of the world not because He's nasty. It's because they are such clowns.

#687
The truth might be unwelcome, unpopular or even outright dangerous but it is never propaganda.

#688
Higher criticism was an attempted autopsy on the living Word.

#689
Satan always charges $1000 for what turns out to be two bucks' worth of stuff.

#690
Sometimes, the wisest way to "embrace who you are" is to put it into a strait jacket.

#691
The tragedies of human character begun in Adam are a result of "answering" our own prayers by force.

#692
The serpentine showdown in Pharaoh's court is what should have happened in Eden.

TESTING

#693
Those "drawn to the fringes of the faith" are
just like Adam. They want all of God's gifts but
are not willing to trust God Himself.

#694
Imagine a soldier who discovers that what he
thought was army life was in fact only bootcamp.
That is the myopia of anyone without Christ.

#695
Seems to me that Total Depravity is not a state of
"cannot" repent but a kind of corporate Adamic
"will not." Thus we are still accountable.

#696
When Adam's spirit departed he returned to dust.
When God's Spirit left the Temple, Gentiles tore it apart.
But Jesus saw no corruption.

#697
Alone with my thoughts again. What a pity we don't get on.

#698
It is distressing that so many wonderful people
never come to Christ. If God's wood shavings
are that good, imagine the finished product.

#699
Without God, it is impossible to get a "camel"
into the kingdom. But without God it is entirely possible
to swallow one. (Matt 19:24; 23:24)

BIRDS OF THE AIR

#700
We know John was a Baptist because he preached like one. It was the Presbyterians who came to question him.

#701
When it came to himself,
A. W. Tozer was a total legalist.
When it came to others, he was a libertarian.

#702
The triune office in Judah's three sons:
Er (Watchman: priest/forming), Onan (Strength: king/filling) & Shelah (Prosperity: prophet/future).

#703
Jesus said, "Call no man your father."
That is why the Orthodox Churches revere Tradition.

#704
Jesus said, "Call no man your teacher." That is why the Church of Rome established the Magisterium.

#705
Jesus engaged men's minds with riddles that could be solved only by faith.

#706
The doctor says I have an acute case of metalepsis.

#707
Seeing the light and walking in the light are different things.

*"Our bones are reclothed with
a new and amorous body."*

— Arthur Rimbaud
(*Being Beauteous*)

MATURITY

#708
Wisdom is disarming not only because it is practical
but also because it is beautiful.

#709
Works are evidence of faith in the same way
that smoke is evidence of a fire.

#710
Blessed are the peacemakers,
but peace is not pacificism.
Solomon was at peace with his enemies –
after he killed or exiled David's enemies.

#711
Nobody ever talked about including
the prophets of Baal in the conversation.

#712
God spoke to Samuel, a child, instead of Eli, High Priest,
as the beginning of judgment upon Eli
(Deut 31:21; Ps 8:2; Is 3:4; Matt 21:16).

#713
As in boxing, the aim in theological debate is not
to convert your opponent but your audience.

#714
When debating, remember the testimony of Moses
was not intended to convert Pharaoh. It was for
the sake of the world and the glory of God.

BIRDS OF THE AIR

#715
Systematic theology is a valley of dry bones.

#716
A woman preaching not only demeans
womanhood, it also demeans men.

#717
Israel was a cell. The Church is a virus.

#718
True Gospel witness is the bubbling over
of the fullness of a believing heart.

#719
"Let me tell you the good news of
Covenant theology," said nobody, ever.

#720
If you talk more about Covenant
than you do about Jesus,
you don't understand Jesus.

#721
Reformed theology is the best school in which to learn
about covenant theology, yet it is also the worst place to
learn about New Covenant theology.

#722
Those who won't learn from the hard words
of God's prophets always end up learning the hard way —
through consequences.

MATURITY

#723
Abraham's seed was Christ. And all Christ's offspring
are Abrahams – they hear the Gospel and believe.

#724
When Jesus gives you a new name it won't be
Stormie, Hershey, Tallon, Quoshanique or Barackeisha.
Or anything with a dash that you pronounce.

#725
The Nazis stole works of art.
The Islamists destroy them.
Imagine being evil AND stupid.

#726
Bad theologians need to think in pictures.
Good theologians need to think in moving pictures.

#727
The Bible, like its prophets, will never be a part of the
establishment since its purpose is to speak to it.

#728
Pagans of all stripes revel in the joy and power of music.
But it is a gift stolen from heaven.
There is no music in hell.

#729
The "Covenant continuity" between Abraham and Christ
is the continuity between flesh and smoke
via the fire of Pentecost: transformation.

BIRDS OF THE AIR

#730
Piracy and privacy legislation began in Eden.
Adam stole from God, then he hid himself,
then he blamed the government.

#731
Hipster Jesus? Jesus was as hip as Jeremiah,
who was decidedly unhip.

#732
The pen is mightier than the sword
because prophets are fathers to kings.

#733
Consensus is when everyone in any field
puts all their eggs in one basket.

#734
The meek will eventually inherit the earth,
but the wicked will always have to buy it.

#735
Be blessed. Skip the gym
and mow a neighbor's lawn instead.

#736
When the king decrees that all the churches
can be plundered, his time is short.

#737
True apostolic succession is a willingness
to be a living sacrifice.

MATURITY

#738
The Left is concerned with theft at the top;
the Right with theft at the bottom. But no one seems
particularly concerned with theft per se.

#739
Yahweh asked Ezekiel to "see" because
He needed two legal witnesses, heaven and earth,
the testimony of a son of man as one of the elohim.

#740
Love and truth are not opposites, and neither exists
without the other. Without love, truth is not truth.
Without truth, love is not love.

#741
The Covenant is no longer administered by servants.
It is now administered by sons.

#742
Someone carries the curse so that history
can move on freely. Someone is bound so that
somebody else may be loosed.

#743
No Christian should describe the nations as "pagans"
without qualifying it with the word "precious."

#744
The only thing worse than someone who doesn't
like repetition in art/music/literature is
someone who can't recognize it.

BIRDS OF THE AIR

#745
If Jesus Himself is the true Israel,
one cannot be a true Jew by physical birth.

#746
Why does God not stop injustice immediately?
Because while He disciplines His children
He allows the wicked to fill up their sins.

#747
Everything to which Joseph put his hand prospered.
Clearly he was a greedy capitalist.

#748
Insisting on an understanding of the NT which
ignores AD70 is like reading the prophets without
reference to Israel's captivity.

#749
Regenerate men and regenerate women
have complementary roles in worship.
This "cultus" plays out prophetically in culture.

#750
Christians serve sacrificially to earn the right to speak.
In Christ, a human life lived, God earned
the right to speak as a fellow man.

#751
The lips, teeth and tongue are the elders
who sit and judge in the gate of the city.

MATURITY

#752
Fighting sin and resting in Christ
are two edges of the same blade.

#753
God tries, exposes and heals our hearts through our trials.
He also tries, exposes and heals our culture
through our testimony.

#754
When I draw a crowd it's almost always a lynch mob.

#755
When the knives come out, the peacemaker
quickly adds forks, napkins, chairs, a table and
a good bottle of wine so nobody has to die.

#756
The heavenly Father gives his children stones for bread
and serpents for fish. The wilderness is transformed
into Land and Sea by faith.

#757
The Spirit guides us into "every kind" of truth,
a united body from a single mind instead of fragments
which cause dichotomies and factions.

#758
The more complicated (not complex) something is,
the more likely it is to have been contrived.

BIRDS OF THE AIR

#759
The fruitful life is a life that is
constantly being beheaded by the truth.

#760
Adam hid behind fig leaves. Cain hid behind
the fruit of the ground. In both cases, restoring
fellowship with God instead required blood.

#761
Hard hearts are a universal challenge, but our culture's
vehement hatred of Christ is tipping towards insanity.
We are a harvest of thorns.

#762
One rarely sees mentioned the Bible verses
about poverty which present it as the inevitable result
of laziness and irresponsibility.

#763
The Gospel era is the age of accountability.
(Acts 17:30)

#764
Gehazi, Elisha's servant, was a type of first century Judah,
which sought the goods of the Gentiles
rather than their good.

#765
John the Baptist gives us a great example
of how to be "relevant" and "engage the culture."

MATURITY

#766
There is no longer any "Covenant" in the Old Testament sense. Instead of words and tablets, there is Jesus and the Spirit.

#767
Paul knew that great suffering led not only to great glory but also great vindication. AD70 was a worldwide proof of the divinity of Christ.

#768
Jesus' resurrection is the center of history.
Jesus' ascension is the center of eternity.

#769
The prophet is a divine mirror who exposes what we cannot see for ourselves.

#770
Jesus bought a glorious resurrection for everyone who believes, but staying dead isn't an option for unbelievers.

#771
Q: "Do you want to reach the unchurched?"
A: That all depends on what "churched" means once they are reached.

#772
The Holy Spirit now seems able to tear down my delusions slightly faster than I can build new ones. This could be a tipping point.

BIRDS OF THE AIR

#773
Like David, the enthroned Christ rules over the prophets and yet makes Himself subject to them. Who are the prophets? His Gospel witnesses.

#774
If we preach the Gospel, we can enjoy the infamy of the scandal for the glory of Christ.

#775
Fallen angels don't sing. But fallen men do. Fallen men can be redeemed.

#776
In Peter's recommission, and in ours, there is a call to sacrificial life. There is a transfixing redness to the New Covenant dawn.

#777
According to Paul, the proof of his circumcised heart was his beaten, scarred body, the marks of Jesus.

#778
Baptism and table are about the believer's testimony to others, not God's testimony to us.

#779
The flesh is wont to be consumed, as artists, addicts, the aged and the amorous know, but known best by the apostles and their fiery Christ.

MATURITY

#780
The failure of the West is not a lack of generosity
but its turning from the source of its prosperity.

#781
Like Samson's glorious hair, growing out of
a bloodied Covenant head, the apostle's strength
was made complete in weakness.

#782
What's with churches called "tabernacles"?
We no longer need either tents or temples
because Christ's Spirit tabernacles in us.

#783
Unconversion: "If there is a God, He is bad."
Conversion: "God is good."
Spiritual maturity: "God is way too good."

#784
When Hebrews mentions a great "cloud of witnesses,"
it may be a sign of our disconnect with the OT that we
never think of fragrant smoke.

#785
Churches are tax exempt because the State is not our god.

#786
"Reimagining church" is one of our New Covenant
freedoms. But we'd best get ourselves a biblical
imagination first.

BIRDS OF THE AIR

#787
"I'm spiritual but not religious" be like
"I'm all dressed up with nowhere to go."

#788
When God hardens people's hearts,
He doesn't do it from the inside.
He does it through the faithful witness of the prophets.

#789
If a strange homeless person asks you for money at church,
tell him you first require a definition of Calvinism.*

#790
In Christ, Paul was able to renounce a doctrine
he had cherished all his life. Even as old men
we must be open to changing our minds.

#791
Through a shedding of immaturity,
leaves and skin,
Man is to outdo both tree and serpent.

#792
Exodus shows us that when rulers abuse the saints
to build their houses, God judges and plunders them
so the saints can rebuild His house.

---

*Based partially upon true events, an internet meme circulated in 2013 in which a pastor disguised himself as a homeless man and visited his new church to assess their welcome and generosity before delivering a sermon.

MATURITY

#793
The sacraments do not make saints.
They are the legal testimony of those who are
already saints: "I follow Christ in voluntary death."

#794
Those who hear the warnings of Christ and are filled
with fear are the ones who have nothing to fear.

#795
Truth is more important than people's feelings.
Truth can be spoken in love, but people's feelings
don't get to change the truth.

#796
Our fiction addiction is comorbid with our itchy ears.

#797
At Ascension, there is singing in heaven.
At Maturity, there is singing on earth.

#798
Western apostasy is not a lunge but a parry;
not an attack but a defense.

#799
Calling the Pharisees a "brood" or "nest" of vipers
was a direct reference to the seed of the serpent.

#800
"My pastor says he is 'broadly complementarian.'"
"Is that why he lets broads preach now and then?"

BIRDS OF THE AIR

#801
Outside Israel, the prophets were heralds of salvation.
Within Israel, they were God's "repo men."
The Christian mission is the same.

#802
Being a living sacrifice means walking around in the fire
and coming out unharmed to testify (Acts 2).

#803
Stalin and Mao cut off the old order by murdering
millions. Christ and His Church cut off the
old order by being murdered.

#804
Job did not need answers from God to be comforted.
All he needed was to see the expression on His face.
(Job 42:5)

#805
Before Christ, animals substituted for people. After Christ,
regenerate people substitute for unregenerate people.

#806
Brian McLaren's smug smile will vaporize when he finds
out it's God judging him, not the other way around.

#807
Nero's burning of Christians at his infamous
garden parties brought the flames of Pentecost to Rome.

MATURITY

#808
Welfare does not work because Man cannot be separated
from his gifts any more than God can.

#809
Unlike paganism, Secularism is "high handed" rebellion,
a revolt against God which is fully informed about Him.

#810
Marriage debate: Church and State running
to catch the ball, each shouting "Mine!"
But the ball belongs to the game.

#811
Marriage of necessity involves both Church and State,
since what goes on behind closed doors
eventually becomes everybody's business.

#812
Today, thousands of people around the world took to
the streets to protest against the weather.

#813
When mission turns to self-preservation instead
of self-sacrifice, in the individual or the institution,
the glory departs.

#814
If you stand theologically on someone else's shoulders,
try not to kick him in the head. But it's okay to
bend an ear now and then.

BIRDS OF THE AIR

#815
The prodigal went out full and returned empty.
He also went out empty and returned full.

#816
Why do U.S. foreign policy and foreign aid
keep backfiring? Because the only truly effective
foreign policy and aid is Gospel missions.

#817
I wonder how many at the judgment will blame lying
teachers who told them exactly what they wanted to hear.

#818
RC Sproul said Satan would get an "A" in his
systematic theology course. But he didn't tell us
which seminaries offered to employ him.

#819
Democracy fails when the voice of the people
becomes the voice of a god.

#820
Scifi gives us aliens to show us by contrast what it is to be
human. Sin gives us same-sex marriage to show us by
contrast what marriage is.

#821
Having Sanctuary access as a believer means
you look into the Ark-tomb and see that it's empty,
and then you go and tell the world.

MATURITY

#822
When you think money is the solution to every problem, Mammon is your God.

#823
The apostolic witness in Jerusalem and in the synagogues across the empire was the final "Hear, O Israel."

#824
A fretful political theology and a fundamentalist cultural retreat are both muddle-headed, just in opposite directions.

#825
When a nation has rejected the Word of God, arguing over where money would be best spent is rearranging the deck chairs on the Titanic.

#826
The Body of Christ is a barracks not a nursery.

#827
Peter was commissioned to feed the sheep and also to lead them to the slaughter – by example.

#828
The Days of Awe: The ten day journey from Sinai to Canaan was included in Israel's calendar as the time between Trumpets and Atonement.

#829
It is the nature of an idolatrous culture to profess to be progressive even as it becomes increasingly backward.

BIRDS OF THE AIR

#830
A spiritual vacuum cannot remain so forever.
When Christ is cast into the wilderness,
He returns with greater power.

#831
It's not wise to ask me a theological question
before I've had my coffee. It's even more foolish
to ask me after I've had my coffee.

#832
Jesus is an eternally fragrant offering.
But His incense is burial spices, not the
Grandma lavender of 19th century pietism.

#833
Some preachers understand the heart of God.
Some preachers understand the heart of man.
Few preachers understand both.

#834
Grumpy old men have lived long enough to grieve
over the flesh and its consequences in the world
but not met its solution in Christ.

#835
The "assumption of Mary" is mere fiction.
Revelation shows us what really happened,
one generation later: the ascension of the Bride.

#836
Martyrdom is the pruning of a fruitful tree.

MATURITY

#837
What adjective are we supposed to use to describe what happens when atheists get "preachy?"

#838
The Old Covenant witnesses under the altar were headless, individually and corporately. Like John, they were a Body awaiting a new Head.

#839
In welfare, the state depersonalizes generosity. In incarceration, it depersonalizes restitution, robbing the offender of generosity's joy.

#840
When Jesus stands at the door and knocks, He's the Covenant sheriff coming to serve Covenant papers. "Come, let us reason together."

#841
The difference between Old Covenant and New Covenant angels is that the new ones take justified flesh back to heaven.

#842
The Body of Moses was the death of the flesh. The Body of Christ is witnesses from the tomb.

#843
INDICTMENT: The secular state is operating on all cylinders, and yet the Christian pulpit remains a safe place to be.

BIRDS OF THE AIR

#844
God gave us two hands: hard work and generosity.
The statist Left also has two hands:
entitlements (laziness) and taxes (theft).

#845
Church and State separation is merely the
differing roles of David and Nathan. Nathan advised
David in private and humiliated him in public.

#846
When the presidential election is a choice between
two corporate raiders, choose the one who can
tell when a company is viable.

#847
What is judgment for sinners is
merely discipline for saints.

#848
The world scoffs at repentance not only because it
never repents but also because it never forgives.

#849
The separation of Church from State is your front door.
If you kick the Church out of your private life,
the State will fill the vacuum.

#850
One difference between Right and Left is
rich people on the Left think you have
too much money and can't be trusted with it.

MATURITY

#851
The suffering of the saints is not the mark
of an irredeemable world but the very means
of its transformation.

#852
For the prophets, language with a double meaning
was a veiled blade. Ambiguous use of a word,
done rightly, is the two-edged dagger of Ehud.

#853
Your response to the Spirit at Pentecost
determines which host you join at Trumpets.
Are you an angel-witness, or is your name "Legion"?

#854
In a blameless death, Jesus wrested the power of death
from the devil. He gives it to His disciples.
We wield our own deaths like a weapon.

#855
True Church unity is the sum of the personal
devotion of Spirit-led individuals, and nothing less,
or it's the wrong kind of compromise.

#856
Priests were authorized to kill substitutionary animals,
kings to execute lawless subjects,
and prophets to cut off entire nations.

#857
Rationalism is more rations than it is rational.

BIRDS OF THE AIR

#858
When Paul asked the Colossians to pray for
an open door, the one he likely had in mind was
the door to a courtroom where he could testify.

#859
Man once sacrificed for a fragrance acceptable to God.
God now offers the fragrance of the perfect sacrifice to men.

#860
In a culture willfully following the path to futility
which Paul warns against in Romans 1,
the absurdum needs less and less reductio.

#861
Noah was perceived as ridiculous.

#862
The servant of the Lord doesn't fight (2 Tim. 2:24).
He goes home and tells his big brother, Jesus.

#863
Christian, you have received "the implanted Word."
It cannot return to God void, but how full will it be?

#864
A democracy can vote to redefine immorality as morality,
but it can't vote to change its consequences.

#865
Free speech is expensive but worth every penny.

MATURITY

#866
Faith is not mere mental assent
because a Covenant is a holy mission.

#867
If God heals you, it's so you can be a miraculous
testimony to others. If he doesn't, it's so you can be a
miraculous testimony to others.

#868
A fearless testimony causes others to fear.

#869
Roman roads were built for the Gospel.
Likewise, Jesus owns the internet.

#870
Gandalf, not theology, is the real reason
good ministers wear white robes.

#871
In some profound heaven-and-earth, Adam-and-Eve way,
knowledge is singular but wisdom is plural.

#872
"Spells and smells" can be wonderful in worship,
but those words and clouds must leave the building
as the Warrior Bride.

#873
For Man, order and beauty are things to be grasped, but
for God, order and beauty are the outcomes of holiness.

BIRDS OF THE AIR

#874
James Jordan was the first Bible teacher I ever heard
who showed me the text as a musical score
instead of a box of jigsaw pieces.

#875
The nakedness of the Last Adam
meant the game of "animal hide" was over.

#876
If we endure faithfully, we bring gravity
with us out of the grave.

#877
The Church is a resurrection body.
Her mediatory role as a royal priesthood is prophetic:
prayer and legal testimony.

#878
The ten Tables and ten Lampstands in
Solomon's Temple were a "Church-State"
bridal couple for each of the Ten Words.

#879
Paul wrote Romans 1 to the prodigal son,
and Romans 2 to his big brother.

#880
The Left Wing thinks the debate is all about how
the pie is going to be cut up. The Right just wants
to be free to build pie factories.

MATURITY

#881
John had locusts and wild honey on his tongue
that it might be a sword to divide between
Hagar and Sarah, Egypt and Canaan.

#882
The Gospel destroys tribal culture. It calls us from
animistic childhood to adulthood. Once the Gospel
wakes you up, the Dreamtime is over.

#883
Jesus fulfilled the Old Covenant, and now
He's fulfilling the New Covenant, by His Spirit, in us.
We are "the righteousness of God" in Him.

#884
Taking every thought captive to Christ binds the mind
but frees the body. This is why Jesus was taken captive –
to free the Body.

#885
The abundance and the life of the "abundant life"
is other people, a harvest that comes from being
a seed that is willing to die.

#886
Risk-free Christianity is miracle-free Christianity.

#887
The drawing of animals to Noah was a witness
against a murderous people. Gentiles being drawn
to Jesus was a similar testimony.

BIRDS OF THE AIR

#888
Of course there are prophetesses! The prophetic
role is "bridal," advisory to the king. That's also
what the Church does for the nations.

#889
As in the climax of "Peter and the Wolf,"
the more the cunning Edomite Fox struggled,
the tighter became the Apostolic rope around its neck.

#890
Like great achievement, enduring art
is usually born of sacrifice.

#891
Jesus won't be ashamed of you because of your sin
but because you failed to be a fearless witness.
Be consumed with the fire of witness.

#892
Jesus ripped into the Pharisees for following
@fakeMoses.

#893
Unlike generosity, welfare is help with no obligation
to pay it forward. Our "gospel" is often the same:
comfort and security for ME.

#894
Which part of "all men will hate you"
do we not understand?

MATURITY

#895
All preachers should have a Scottish accent.

#896
The flaming sword with which Adam was to
destroy the serpent was his tongue,
speaking the Words of God.

#897
Evangelicalism is exposed in its music lyrics:
worldwide but an inch deep.

#898
Why did the Jews suppose that the disciples were drunk?
Because they were bold and loud,
and alcohol loosens tongues.

#899
God doesn't bless many of His children
with enormous earthly riches because He
doesn't want to spoil them for the real stuff.

#900
I'm thankful for Christians who can challenge
the great philosophers, but why must they use
big words to describe such ground level ideas?

#901
First, we are holy to avoid judgment.
Then, we are holy because we love Christ.
Finally, we realize holiness is also a spiritual weapon.

BIRDS OF THE AIR

#902
Perhaps the reason some traditions get persnickety about priestly vestments is their failure to understand baptism as prophetic investiture.

#903
Western Christians are asleep because they are fed milk and taught lullabies.

#904
Jesus doesn't care about the visible/invisible church distinction. The true church is the audible church: witnesses to the resurrection.

#905
The Law of Moses is the Law for Priests.
The Sermon on the Mount is the Law for Kings.
The Spirit Himself is the Law for Prophets.

#906
God's face is against you (Altar-Priest),
then His face shines upon you (Fire-King),
and then HE MAKES YOU HIS FACE (Smoke-Prophet)

#907
In the Bible, donkeys are to horses as grasshoppers are to locusts.

#908
A parable is a two-edge sword, spoken to divide the people.
Then that Word is made flesh:
the righteous are gathered; the wicked are slain.

MATURITY

#909
Christians are often bullied at school.
There should be government-funded programs
explaining Christianity to the hagiophobes.

#910
If a preterist view of the Revelation is anti-Semitic,
then the book of Ezekiel is also anti-Semitic.

#911
Communism was a real threat only because many of its
proponents were willing to die for their cause.

#912
To deny Christ is to fail to testify.
To deny oneself is to testify to Christ.

#913
Sharing your faith isn't a transmission of data.
It's a formal introduction to a Person.

#914
Paul's "trials" weren't the apostle just getting
through life. His was Covenant suffering after
he took up the cross as a legal witness.

#915
In the Trinity, there is no taking, only receiving.

#916
Morality, like economics, can only be protected,
not determined, by the state.

BIRDS OF THE AIR

#917
The answer to crony capitalism is not socialism.
Socialism doesn't need the word crony before it.
Cronies come with it as a package.

#918
Listen to your elders. But then do what's right.

#919
A revival of interest in great Christian literature
should flow from a revival of love for the Bible,
not become a substitute for it.

#920
The answer to the epidemic of mental illnesses
is not more money for counseling and other services.
It is Christ.

#921
Judas, not Jesus, was the first socialist.

#922
Socialism disguises itself as generosity. Just like the
serpent, it encourages envy and theft in its lust for power.

#923
Based on the Old Testament Covenant patterns,
the defining characteristic of the Church is
prophetic witness, that is, legal testimony.

#924
Liturgy is food and commerce as high art.

MATURITY

#925
Egypt's gods were toppled when the nation was plagued and plundered. It makes sense that the Philistines fashioned plagues out of plunder.

#926
I sometimes pray on one knee
to remind myself I'm not a beggar but an adopted son and willing representative: a priest-king.

#927
Two things amaze me concerning the worldly:
their wisdom and their utter futility.
Both are gifts from God for the saints.

#928
The prophet not only saw God but,
as the representative of the Bride,
communicated intimately, that is, "mouth to mouth."

#929
Vexting: Pronouncing Covenant imprecations by SMS.

#930
Why do all the well-known preachers keep twittering the bleeding obvious? Solomon never did. Neither did Jesus.

#931
When atheists are defending a worldview that allows men to be lawless, they sound just like preachers.

BIRDS OF THE AIR

#932
If the Psalms feel out of place in your worship service, imagine how Jesus feels.

#933
Secularists now understand the benefits of gratitude, but to whom/what are they thankful? This monstrous idolatry steals gratitude itself.

#934
Beer drinking and pipe smoking will get you facedown and covered in ashes. But wouldn't you rather be remembered for your prayer life?

#935
Let your preaching be an alluring glimpse into the Bible's worldview. Speak as God does from the cloud: glorious, inviting and bulletproof.

#936
In the prophets, Yahweh concerns Himself not only with Israel but also with Gentiles. This makes the prophets more relevant, not less.

#937
The New Covenant "Tree" of Life (Rev 22:2) and "Fruit" of the Spirit are singular, not plural, because they represent a new "kind."

#938
In Jesus, the burial spices of a 500 year Winter came out of the earth as an eternally fragrant Spring.

MATURITY

#939
According to Revelation 8:1, rightly interpreted,
the continuous singing of angels in heaven
was stopped while the apostles preached.

#940
What's the good of "evangelicalism"
if it doesn't evangelize?
When did you last testify for Jesus?

#941
When Jesus suffered He was in total control
of the situation. When the Church suffers she is in
total control of the situation (Rev. 2:27).

#942
Picasso did not paint for the eyes but the gut.
He painted for the gut that the eyes might be opened.

#943
The reason we cannot envisage corporate or civic
repentance today is because it is always a miracle.

#944
Perhaps if we comprehended the text as the ravishing
music it is, we would have less trouble singing along.

#945
Socialists are like the childless child expert who tells you
how to raise your kids. What do they know?
They never produced anything.

BIRDS OF THE AIR

#946
Forgive us our debt crisis, as we forgive those who borrowed money for overpriced student loans.

#947
Pastor, if you're a little bit country,
I'm a little bit Steve Reich.

#948
Prophets never let their targets set the agenda.
Proclaim the grace and glory of Christ
and all objections are silenced.

#949
Jesus spoke in riddles and parables
because He was a veil to be torn (Heb. 10).
By the Spirit, He is now the open door.

#950
Jesus' blood covered the believers, but we must never forget that His blood was also avenged upon those who refused to believe.

#951
Jesus said He would build His Church. Why do we act like He merely gave us the instructions?

#952
The seal of the Spirit is not something to
"keep me safe until heaven."
It is the seal on a Gospel scroll to be broken.

MATURITY

#953
The blood no longer calls down curses, crying from the ground. It advocates for us in heaven, speaking better things than the blood of Abel.

#954
He from whose body flowed blood and water
would stand on the Land and the Sea
and unite them as one new Man.

#955
Paul's cosmopolitan background was the epitome
of the mystery of Christ, the union of Jew and Gentile
in one new man.

#956
The problem with having a mind like a buzz saw is it sometimes sticks out your mouth and hurts people.

#957
Many of the best books in history
were written on tobacco leaves.

#958
The conversation at God's table is for those who know their Master's mind, who hear His voice as children and thus quit themselves like men.

#959
Secularists love to point out the wheezing "death rattles"
in the Western Church, unaware of the fact
that this Church is their own lungs.

BIRDS OF THE AIR

#960
Israel was healed by Jesus' stripes, but her deliverance involved rubbing His salty words into her wounds at the hand of the Apostles.

#961
Facts are things which we can collect and store, but the truth is something which possesses us.

#962
So often, what mainstream churches identify as "numinous" is just plain old nebulous.

#963
Mozart was able to take a pre-existing artistic form, inhabit it entirely, and revolutionize it from the inside. Much like Jesus in John 1.

#964
We worship a God for whom even judgment is a song.

Noah's wife: "Is it the wind which waileth?"
Noah: "No wife. It is the chaff
which the wind driveth away."

— JOHN HUSTON'S 'THE BIBLE' (1966)

CONQUEST

#965
For the people of God, the "last days" are
only ever the last days of the old order.

#966
Unlike the chariot of Pharaoh, the arrival of the chariot
of God brings not only vengeance but also redemption.

#967
Waving or worshiping rainbows isn't going to protect
anybody from the baptismal flood of the Church.

#968
Without fail, glorying in the Church and the
sacraments turns her into a harlot. It is only glorying
in Christ which gathers the Church.

#969
If the Dominion mandate (Forming) was repeated
in the Great Commission (Filling), Philip would have
given the eunuch his testicles back.

#970
Paedobaptism is just the downstream version
of baptism for the dead.

#971
Paedobaptism (bap-cision) isn't deliverance from stoicheia.
Bap-cision is a relic of the stoicheia we were delivered from.

#972
Giving wine to infants puts the mental in sacramentalism.

BIRDS OF THE AIR

#973
We don't gather, confess sins, hear the Word,
sing Psalms or take Communion to appease God.
We do it because He has been appeased in Christ.

#974
Christians are the light of the world and the salt of the
earth. Plenty of light and salt in Sodom (Gen 19:11; 19:26).

#975
Moses executed an Egyptian as a righteous judge,
but Israel rejected him. 40 years later he returned
"in like manner" and slew more.

#976
At the climax of next Sunday's service, the communion
bread will be delivered to us by trained ravens.

#977
As my understanding and terror of God's wrath
increases, so does my wonder at His love for me
and the fact that I am entirely free from it.

#978
"Covenant blessings" no longer exist. There is only Jesus.
Don't depersonalize Him. Use His name, please.

#979
Baptist culture proves the price of ignorance,
but paedobaptist doctrine proves that a little knowledge
is a dangerous thing.

CONQUEST

#980
"Baptize the nations" didn't mean put them
under obligation to Christ, since they already were.
He said, "Now you can baptize Gentiles, too."

#981
Circumcision was about preventing a repeat of
Cain and Abel in Canaan and Shem. Baptism is about
Adam and Eve. Very different.

#982
Paedobaptists say "fruit checking" children before
baptism is fraught with uncertainty, then use exactly
the same standards on adults.

#983
If your cause is not godly, that giddy feeling when
you cross the finish line might be the last spin
of your barrel going over the falls.

#984
Sacramentalists don't do door knocking.
Telling people they need an impersonal relationship
with Jesus doesn't go down too well.

#985
As we become living sacrifices,
the Sacraments take on flesh.

#986
Paedobaptism is the magical name-it-and-claim-it
of Reformed theology. Just saying.

BIRDS OF THE AIR

#987
The New Covenant sign is not about obligation
but transformation. People don't enter the church.
They become the church.

#988
Jesus fulfilled Israel. There is no "Covenant people."
There is only Jesus. You are regenerate and in Him,
or merely generate and outside.

#989
The point of the "household baptisms" was not infants.
It signified the Covenant was moving from the sons of
Abraham to the sons of God.

#990
Baptism concerns the Covenant Oath
(submission before heaven), but circumcision
concerned the Sanctions (inheritance on earth).

#991
Under a Melchizedekian priesthood (a priesthood
of all nations, not just one), no sign upon infants was,
or is, either given or required.

#992
Christ crushed the serpent underfoot,
but only the totus Christus has a footprint big enough
to crush the dragon, the totus diabolus.

CONQUEST

#993
In our culture children are murdered, neglected and corrupted. But twisting the New Covenant into a fertility cult is not the answer.

#994
In many Baptist churches, adults drink grape juice. In some Reformed churches, babies drink wine. Is everybody stupid?

#995
The baptism debate hinges on whether baptism places people under Christ's sacrificial authority or gives them that authority.

#996
Circumcision was the sign of a curse transformed into blessings. Baptism is delegated authority to curse and to bless.

#997
Baptism is not a sign that one is under Covenant guardians but that one is now an authorized Covenant guardian.

#998
Every Covenant is a forming and a filling with a promised future. As one, the Old is forming (1st birth) and the New is filling (2nd birth).

#999
Every baptism is the "end of Egypt." But make sure you use enough to water to drown at least one Egyptian.

BIRDS OF THE AIR

#1000
0 = How much evidence for paedosacraments the Bereans found when they searched the Scriptures.

#1001
All Israel was baptized into Moses the Prophet. Now all the Lord's people are prophets like Moses, baptized individually. (Numbers 11:29)

#1002
I have nothing against paedosacraments. The question is whose children are we talking about: the sons of men or the sons of God? (Jn 1:13)

#1003
The world sees Christianity as a merely social or cultural phenomenon rather than a supernatural one. Our baptisms should refute this.

#1004
The "second death" alludes to the second goat, doomed to carry sin: earthly Israel. The "first death" was the martyrs who ascended to God.

#1005
Only the second-born are safe from the second death.

#1006
Salvation is certainly a process, but as with any citizenship, there is a watershed moment before which you are not and after which you are.

CONQUEST

#1007
To define "Covenant child" in New Covenant terms, look no further than Jesus' baptism where the Son's obedient faith pleased the Father.

#1008
Paedofaith is like the New Testament but with midichlorians.

#1009
If you discovered after its baptism that your infant was swapped at birth, and you then swapped it back, was the baptism efficacious?

#1010
Getting a confession: Is waterboarding "objective Covenant" done Baptist-style?

#1011
The birds of the air chased away by Abraham now feed his prophets a blessing instead of bringing us a curse.

#1012
Credobaptism excludes no one from "the Covenant." The end of circumcision means nobody's outside it. Baptism is just a uniform for the staff.

#1013
If we desisted from infant baptism, what would happen? Nothing. If we desisted from believer's baptism? Europe.

BIRDS OF THE AIR

#1014
In the choice of Christ from among repentant Jews at His baptism, circumcision of the flesh was cut off, leaving only that of the heart.

#1015
God isn't interested in sons of Abraham. He is interested in those who are sons of God like Abraham – spiritual offspring by the Gospel.

#1016
I'm a credobaptist because I applied the pattern of Covenant Renewal Worship to the individual saint as a living sacrifice: ordo sacrificii.

#1017
As in Eden, atonement was an unfair barter, an unequal exchange, in which God was happy to be ripped off.

#1018
Jews wait for Messiah's first coming and Christians wait for His second. But these were the double approach of the High Priest at Atonement.

#1019
The Word of the Lord never returns to Him empty, even when that Word is a ravenous curse.

#1020
Israel was baptized as ONE: a body of flesh. The Church is baptized as MANY: a cloud of smoke.

CONQUEST

#1021
In the Eucharist, the Church militant consumes
all flesh and all blood: every land and every people.
Hereditary membership is out of place.

#1022
Sacramentalism mistakes baptism and table for means of
future salvation rather than testimonies of something
which has already occurred.

#1023
All Israel was baptized in one go. Christians are baptized
one by one. That means there is a distinct element of
individualism in salvation.

#1024
Credobaptism is not inherently individualistic.
In baptism, the individual willingly joins a physical
but regenerate BODY.

#1025
Every claim of divine sonship outside of circumcision
of heart is by definition a work of the devil.

#1026
A baptism which does not discern between
the fruit of the womb and the fruit of the tomb
is anti-Christ, denying He has come in the flesh.

#1027
The Lord can't judge every man according to his works
because that would be individualism.

BIRDS OF THE AIR

#1028
Church discipline is for discerning the names in the book of life, not for overplaying or undermining assurance.

#1029
Revelation never names the "great city" as Jerusalem. She was no longer the city of peace but Egypt (Galatians 4:25) and Sodom (2 Peter 2:6).

#1030
God already has your #snapchat photos for His case against you. Turn to Christ.

#1031
Sorry to confuse you. When I mentioned "the great unwashed" I was referring to Reformed Theology.

#1032
Paedobaptism is Abrahamic foosball in the clubhouse. The real game is with Jesus, out there on the field.

#1033
I will ask the Father and he will give you a Helper, even the Sociology of the Church, which the world cannot receive. #thingsjesusneversaid

---

#1034
"Go get people baptized as Covenant members so you can preach the Gospel to them." #thingsjesusneversaid

CONQUEST

#1035
When smart theologians say ludicrous things,
there's always a wrong turn in their logic a few steps back
– usually at the baptismal font.

#1036
ICHABOD: At the cross, Christ gave up
His last breath. A generation later,
the Spirit left Jerusalem's Temple desolate.

#1037
Jesus' baptism: authority to speak WORD
Jesus' transfiguration: authority to die SACRAMENT
Jesus' ascension: authority to rule GOVERNMENT

#1038
Pietists treat the saved like they are lost. Sacramentalists treat the lost like they are saved. Both are control freaks.

#1039
A PDF is the only place I would ever embed a font.

#1040
The phrase "pulling yourself up by your baptism"
is the soteriological equivalent
of the bootstrap paradox.

#1041
Paedobaptism assumes the Church is on the defensive.
Credobaptism assumes the Church is on the offensive.
One of these is wrong.

BIRDS OF THE AIR

#1042
Sinner, you think the NSA has all your personal info?
Wait till you see what God's got on you.

#1043
Just as Circumcision made impossible a global corruption,
so paedobaptism makes impossible a global Gospel.

#1044
The Covenant Oath was not about circumcision
of the flesh but of the heart. The Law was objective,
but the Mosaic Covenant was not.

#1045
Circumcision was about conquest of the Land.
Baptism is about conquest of the Sea.

#1046
The bronze laver was a "lake of fire,"
like the words and tears of a prophet:
cleansing for some and destruction for others.

#1047
Paedobaptism is an assumption that relies on the same
brand of contrived exegesis as the Assumption of Mary.

#1048
The difference between good rain and the Flood
is that between Pentecost and Holocaust.*

---

*Holocaust derives from the name for an offering burnt completely on an altar. Here it refers to the destruction of Jerusalem and Herod's Temple in AD70.

CONQUEST

#1049
The flood was the ultimate in "external law."
Pentecost was the ultimate in "internal law."

#1050
He who defeats the nachash wears the tachash.

#1051
Paedobaptism and same-sex marriage
both use "inclusiveness" as an excuse to rob
a sacred rite of its meaning.

#1052
Confronted with John's and Jesus' call for personal
repentance and faith ratified by public confession in
baptism, the Jews pled "Covenant."

#1053
Jesus' baptism didn't make life easier. It painted
a big red target on Him and cast Him
into the wilderness. It was the same for Paul, too.

#1054
In AD64, the completion of Herod's temple and
Nero's persecution of Christians proved without doubt
that Christ was a false prophet. Or not.

#1055
Paedobaptism is a social baptism, natural rather
than spiritual. Credobaptism can be similarly distorted,
though less easily.

BIRDS OF THE AIR

#1056
Believer's baptism says, "I am your brother," or "I am your sister," not "I am your child." It is about brotherhood in Christ, not parenting.

#1057
Arguing for efficacy of sacraments is fine, but first we must have a biblical understanding of what they do and what they are for.

#1058
Unity of sacrament is the result of unity in Spirit, not its source.

#1059
The Eucharist is not spiritual nourishment. It is a public testimony that, like Jesus, voluntary obedience is our food.

#1060
Most terrible for the lost is that they won't be judged by God but by a sinless human being; moreover, the sinless Man who died for them.

#1061
Paedobaptism has one thing in common with same-sex marriage: you end up redefining everything else just to accommodate it.

#1062
Forcing Revelation 20 into AD70 (full preterism) is as simple as putting a condom on a Zeppelin.

CONQUEST

#1063
Jesus celebrated Passover not with a household but with
legal representatives. This was a table on a mountain.

#1064
In representative terms, the people of God are
no longer the Land but the heavenly Sea.
The Church herself is the oncoming storm.

#1065
AD70 was the expulsion of Judas from the Lord's Table
played out on an imperial scale.

#1066
The whole point of credobaptism is that it allows
the gospel to go VIRAL. Paedobaptism/paedocommunion
locks it up into Adamic family cells.

#1067
"Baptism saves you..." (1 Peter 3:21)
From what did it "deliver" these believing Jews?
Obligation to the Law and its imminent curses.

#1068
A baptism with no repentance
stitches a dead limb onto a living body.

#1069
Paedobaptists expect an Abrahamic inheritance.
Credobaptists understand that WE ARE that inheritance.

BIRDS OF THE AIR

#1070
Baptism is the act of stepping off your parents'/guardians' coat tails because you now have your own.

#1071
What good is reuniting baptism and communion if this reunion divorces them both from the new birth?

#1072
Doug Wilson: "Salvation extends to the world by generational blessing and promise." Wrong. Salvation WAS EXTENDED to the world in that way.

#1073
The pen is mightier than the sword because the Church always rises from the dead.

#1074
Paedobaptism baptizes in hope. Credobaptism baptizes in hope. But they are very different hopes.

#1075
Circumcision made Israel a target. Baptism places Christians as arrows into a quiver.

#1076
For those who believe, all curses become a means of blessing.

#1077
In the last days of each Covenant administration, those who "overcome" do so by being overcome.

CONQUEST

#1078
Under the Abrahamic Covenant, Gentile troops were a flood of judgment. Under Christ, baptized believers are an oncoming flood of life.

#1079
If you believe that Jesus relates to His people by Covenant, then you believe that the Mediator needs a mediator.

#1080
On the last day, there will be no excuses. Even the deepest secrets of God were hidden in plain sight.

#1081
"Come out of her, my people" was not a call to come out of a womb but a tomb. Judah was a whited sepulcher, and he was being born again.

#1082
Pomegranate: a fruit (Adam-priest) which produces a flower (Eve-people). It ripens around the Day of Atonement.

#1083
Jesus' garment's hem is a circle of pomegranates and bells, that is, a border of death and resurrection, a rhythm of sacrifice and praise.

#1084
The "testimony of Jesus Christ" in baptism is a Covenant oath, the answer of the baptizand's good conscience towards God. (1 Peter 3:21)

BIRDS OF THE AIR

#1085
Sacramentalism evades the necessity of hearing the Gospel: Those who hear and believe BECOME the bread and wine and the living water.

#1086
Discussing baptism with a paedobaptist is like discussing Jesus with a Mormon. The word means something entirely different in their minds.

#1087
B.C. was the age of progeny, "seed."
A.D. is the age of recruitment, "harvest."
Communists, gays and Muslims get this.
Paedobaptists don't.

#1088
Paedobaptism makes our physical offspring the "children of God" and "heirs" of the kingdom. It's Judaism revived.

#1089
The power of the accuser is the stigma of sin. In Christ, prostitutes and publicans, and even failed disciples, can lift up their heads.

#1090
Like God's throne, Adam's throne was surrounded by beasts. If he was faithful, they would submit and come to him for shelter.

CONQUEST

#1091
Baptists neglect their children for evangelism.
Paedobaptists think evangelism is their children.

#1092
Claiming unity of Spirit based upon "one baptism"
is fine as long as it's the baptism Paul had in mind.

#1093
Contrary to many, paedobaptism, not credobaptism, is a
sign of the cultural retreat of the Church. Think about it.

#1094
The Shekinah standing in judgment between the pillars
at the Temple threshold should remind us of
Samson just before his departure.

#1095
The answer to life, the universe and everything
is actually 490. (Matthew 18:21-22)

#1096
There is no rivalry between the gospel and the
sacraments, any more than there is between the
wedding invitation and the table place name.

#1097
Despite the recent growth in the popularity of
posthumous pardons, there won't be any from
the court that matters most.

BIRDS OF THE AIR

#1098
Presenting ourselves boldly before God's throne means we esteem Jesus' advocacy as the Father does. We feel safe, which honors Christ.

#1099
Paedosacraments turn the Lord's Supper into kiddies' dinner time rather than the table where God's ambassadors "taste death for every man."

#1100
Baptism by sprinkling is as ineffectual in "cutting off all flesh" as a local flood.

#1101
Until evangelicals take the significance of AD70 into account, much of what the apostles wrote will remain a mystery to them.

#1102
Baptism vindicates the work of the Spirit – internal law, self-government. Church discipline is a reversion to external law.

#1103
The division of physical offspring into two classes of people ended with Herod's Temple.

#1104
Time has a habit of exposing religions, ideologies, individuals and nations for what they really are.

CONQUEST

#1105
Increasing epistemological awareness means that when Jesus returns nearly all remaining sin will be conscious rebellion – high-handed sin.

#1106
Paedobaptism is redundant because the only blessing it could possibly confer is already given to all children, all people, all nations.

#1107
Your church/denomination are an expression of your service, NEVER an object of your loyalty. Your loyalty is to Christ and His Word.

#1108
The Pharisees criticized Jesus for socializing with publicans and harlots. But Revelation exposes Jerusalem as the archetype of both.

#1109
Jesus was judged and vindicated in the Garden, His name judged and vindicated in the Land. The jury is still out in the World.

#1110
Lent? Even Israel was only called to afflict herself for one day a year.

#1111
Should a man open the door for a woman? Did Jesus open the door for His Bride?

BIRDS OF THE AIR

#1112
An uncircumcised Israel was circumcised outside Jericho before it fell. An uncircumcised Church was martyred outside Jerusalem before it fell.

#1113
Baptists are right about baptism in the way a stopped clock is right twice a day.

#1114
Adam's failed "second birth" brought a curse on all first births. Abraham's "second birth" removed the curse on Sarah's first birth.

#1115
Baptism isn't Jesus' claim on your life. He's already claimed every life. Baptism is your public claim on His life, His name in your mouth.

#1116
The top of every ideological mountain which men build to climb will be covered in a baptismal flood.

#1117
Israel was not destroyed by Babylon and Rome because she was Jewish.
It was because she was not Jewish enough.

#1118
By the time Rome invaded, all the pots and pans in the world were holy, but the Temple bowls were vessels of destruction. (2 Peter 3:10)

CONQUEST

#1119
"Forgive us our sins as we forgive others" is not a conditional threat. It's a description of mediation.

#1120
The pouring out of Jesus' blood on the Land began the dissolution of bloodlines and territories.

#1121
The Bible ends before the destruction of Jerusalem because the Torah ends before the destruction of Jericho.

#1122
When the "Land" was divided in Genesis 10:25, was it a global version of the division of the Land for the tribes under Joshua?

#1123
Like Abraham, those who overcame harlot Jerusalem would be given new names. And Jerusalem was given old names: Sodom, Egypt, Babylon.

#1124
Probably the next worst thing for the unrepentant to facing the image of God in Jesus will be the revelation of the image of God in himself.

#1125
God is preparing us to judge angels, just as He prepared Adam to judge an angel. But we have a better Adam.

BIRDS OF THE AIR

#1126
The Gospel without the rest of the Bible is like
a spearhead attack with no subsequent occupation.

#1127
How do we know John was the Baptist?
Because he preached like one.

#1128
In Revelation 5, Jesus is not holding
divorce papers FOR Israel. He IS Israel,
and He opens His legal claim upon all nations.

#1129
The priests could not throw Temple leftovers to the dogs,
but only unclean meat. Like Jezebel.

#1130
In Zechariah 4, the cherubim that exiled Judah from the
Garden-Land have hammered their flaming swords into
flaming plowshares.

#1131
The words that seal each man's eternal destiny
will be spoken by an enthroned Man.

#1132
Those who will not be purified
by the mercy of heaven
will be purified from the earth.

*"No one can live without delight,
and that is why a man deprived of spiritual joy
goes over to carnal pleasure."*

— St. Thomas Aquinas

GLORIFICATION

#1133
In the toolbox of Creation, alcohol is a powersaw.

#1134
If we're not surprised the sexual revolution became a meat market, we can't complain when it becomes an abattoir.

#1135
Getting a bit tired of experiencing culture shock in my own culture.

#1136
Anything new in theology should be regarded with suspicion. But that does not include all the old stuff we never noticed before.

#1137
Those who come to the Church for shelter are themselves destined to become shelter.

#1138
The "progressive" worldview is like AM radio. They no longer have the moral or historical bandwidth to even comprehend conservative values.

#1139
The disintegration and corruption apparent in Western culture are withdrawal symptoms: the withdrawal of God.

#1140
Judges cannot legislate rightly for human beings if they refuse to believe that human beings are images of God.

BIRDS OF THE AIR

#1141
Seeking to be superhuman, or trans-human,
outside of obedience to God, has always led to
sub-humanity and inhumanity.

#1142
Islam and Secularism are not only the enemies
of the Gospel, they are the results of the Gospel.

#1143
Racism and same-sex marriage are both
attacks on what it means to be human.

#1144
Whether it comes sooner or later, as a Christian
your death is the destruction of your last enemy.

#1145
First Things is holding a 2 day intellectual retreat.
Baptists seem to be ending one which has lasted
half a century or more.

#1146
As a culture turns from God, its art
becomes more symptom than expression,
and criticism more diagnosis than appreciation.

#1147
So much highbrow theology reminds me of
rattling on to fill up the word count in an exam essay
when I didn't really understand the question.

GLORIFICATION

#1148
TV shows get axed when they jump the shark.
Politicians get elected.

#1149
A career politician is somebody who can break
all Ten Commandments regularly, with impunity,
and worse, with sanctimony.

#1150
Secular "values" are being sanctimoniously imposed
upon Christians because those who walk in darkness
see their "truth" as self-evident.

#1151
What the West needs is leaders who promise health
and prosperity if we stop lying, stealing,
sleeping around and murdering babies.

#1152
"Pro choice" is a strange name for people who
(mostly) have demonstrated that they are incapable
of making responsible decisions.

#1153
Why do Americans write MM-DD-YY
instead of DD-MM-YY like the rest of humanity?
It's like Land-Garden-World.

#1154
The problem with "rewriting" the social narrative
is that you can't change the ending.

BIRDS OF THE AIR

#1155
No marriage, no children. No children, no history.
This social experiment will be short lived.

#1156
Contrary to some recent reports, the fundamental cultural strategy of the New Covenant is not Christian parenting.

#1157
Secularism apart from the shelter of Christianity
is a fenceless playground without a school.

#1158
The Apocalypse is the entire Old Testament exposed
in a thousand naphtha flashes on a single frame.
All things came upon that generation.

#1159
Israel's "frontline ministry" was the Feast of Booths,
that is, hospitality and generosity.

#1160
Infants were promised to Adam, but they weren't
tested in the Garden. That's the difference between
circumcision and baptism.

#1161
In the Great Commission, Jesus told His disciples
that their "Covenant community" was no longer "in here"
but "out there." And so is ours.

GLORIFICATION

#1162
They introduced emoticons so we could avoid misunderstandings in text communications. But then I started using emoticons sarcastically.

#1163
Because they are satanic, Islam's legalism and atheism's license both lead to violence against the weak, especially women and children.

#1164
Same-sex marriage debate looks promising to some but is merely an unpleasant vapor (Isaiah 26:18), gas from a corpse. It will come to pass.

#1165
It's telling that the same-sex marriage debate itself needs a safe space to protect it from reality.

#1166
Secularism condemns greed but condones envy and theft. It condemns murder but sacralizes abortion. Rejecting God brings confusion.

#1167
I love professional team sports.
They keep boring people busy.

#1168
Jesus has ERH in Heaven's library of the ages.
But He uses RHE to paper under the kitty litter.*

---

*Eugen Rosenstock-Huessy and Rachel Held Evans.

BIRDS OF THE AIR

#1169
Certainly, the New Covenant has an objective aspect.
All people were included without being asked.
It is the response which is subjective.

#1170
One day, those linear eschatology charts will be a thing
of the past. They simply cannot express what is going on.
God works in fractals.

#1171
Writing for theologians is difficult.
I have to explain everything from scratch.

#1172
If Joe Rogan became a Christian he would be Mark Driscoll.

#1173
Red letter Christianity is like Rome without any roads.

#1174
The cleverest, best-looking, highest-achieving,
self-made preachers are usually theological dopes.

#1175
Reformed+Baptist is the perfect marriage
of biblical logic and spiritual intuition.

#1176
In the Bible, youth leaders are called parents.

GLORIFICATION

#1177
Conservatism works to ensure equal opportunity for all.
Progressivism works to ensure equal outcomes for all.
One of these is stupid.

#1178
The fact that many politicians pretend to be Christians
is not something to rejoice in.
The fact that they still feel the need to is.

#1179
I guess if we can have feminist theology,
and gay theology, we can have atheist theology.

#1180
The claim that abortion is a birthright
is self-evidently delusional.

#1181
Jacob's first son was named "a son" (Initiation).
His last son was named "a son at my right hand"
(Representation).

#1182
Secularism is an autoimmune disease. Only a culture
bent on self destruction vilifies Christianity while
pandering to Islam and immorality.

#1183
Muslims and secularists both suffer from delusions
of entitlement. But only those who submit to Christ
will inherit the earth.

BIRDS OF THE AIR

#1184
Multiculturalists are only just now realizing
that Islam is not multicultural.

#1185
If radical Islam were a video game, it would
beat the pants off Grand Theft Auto.

#1186
The only sinless person in the Koran is Jesus.

#1187
Islam can only survive as a parasite within the
disintegrating corpse of the first Christendom.

#1188
Like Bruce Jenner, Western culture was a winner,
but then self-identified as a biological accident,
and is now going through with the op.

#1189
Note to progressives: The solution to racial divisions
is not the glorification of racial divisions.

#1190
A spiritual problem does not have a political solution.

#1191
For the religious some things are sacred.
For the atheist nothing is sacred. For Christians,
nothing is sacred because everything is sacred.

GLORIFICATION

#1192
God's solution to the intermarriage
with paganism in Genesis 6 was to call a man
and his sons who had all married believers.

#1193
The marital bed is where Bridegroom and Bride
die to themselves, sleep, and rise again as one flesh.

#1194
The love or hatred of Christ is always personal.
The last judgment will likewise be
personal, spoken by human lips.

#1195
There is no longer any Covenant with men.
There is only the Man.

#1196
The Bible Matrix doesn't "steamroll" over text or doctrine.
It shows us where the road actually goes.

#1197
A blog is a man's best friend.

#1198
Typology is not linear but fractalline.
This is why one man can die for many.

#1199
"Covenant" is big government in the
ecclesiological sphere.

BIRDS OF THE AIR

#1200
Only after Jesus lived a blameless life on earth,
womb to tomb, beginning to end, could He be
both our Alpha and our Omega in heaven.

#1201
Secular Conservatism is a process of embalming,
or even taxidermy. Call it Preservatism.

#1202
The celebrity preacher culture is certainly flawed,
but in mainline denominations the top guys
are just world class administrators.

#1203
Obama's second term was entirely necessary.
The Obsurdum required a Reductio.

#1204
Our culture's "remedy" for the failure of men
to lay down freedoms for women is women's refusal
to lay down their freedoms for children.

#1205
The exposure of the sale of baby parts
has not been good for Godwin's Law.

#1206
Gay culture has been the leader in fashion, art,
music and sexual practices since the early 60s.
All anyone under 50 remembers is gay.

GLORIFICATION

#1207
Gay people want complete affirmation because without it they are without hope, and they are without hope because they reject the Gospel.

#1208
In an age when technology brings channels of communication crying out for quality content, our culture has nothing more to say.

#1209
Ironically, the idea that God still has a "carnal" plan for "carnal" Israel is debunked by the Hebraic heartbeat of the apostolic writings.

#1210
The entry parade of Olympic opening ceremonies is a glimpse of the nations at the resurrection. But the glory will all be Christ's.

#1211
Contra Augustine, the world is not reconciled in the Church but in Christ. The Church IS the world reconciled.

#1212
Democracy works until the day every voter thinks like a tyrant.

#1213
The pen is mightier than the sword because it dictates the end rather than the means.

BIRDS OF THE AIR

#1214
In any centuries-old theological dispute where
a plausible case exists on both sides,
the most likely solution is a third way.

#1215
There is no such thing as an overnight success,
but success, when it finally arrives,
usually does so overnight.

#1216
The first laugh was God's. The last will be His also.

#1217
There's a big difference between knowing history and
understanding history. The same goes for the the Bible.

#1218
The Bible works on many levels. If you look carefully,
there are buttons for heights beyond the Ground Floor.

#1219
The awkward moment when you discover One Hour of
Soviet Anthems on your 12 year old son's iPod.

#1220
"Mum, Dad, I've got something to tell you.
I'm a preterist."
"What will we tell the family?"

GLORIFICATION

#1221
Empty seats at Church is temporary.
Empty seats in Heaven is tragedy.

#1222
There is an inverse ratio between the truth of a subject/science/philosophy and the bankrolling/sophistry/coercion required to maintain it.

#1223
Biblical theology is the mathematics of the poet.

#1224
For theology, as it is with mathematics,
the world will soon be a single country.

#1225
The "fractal" literature of the Scriptures is a
divine marriage of mathematical method
and poetic playfulness: structure and glory.

#1226
Institutional theology not only guards against heresy
and innovation, it also guards against the Bible.

#1227
When the bull means business, check whether
you are dealing with the front end or the back end,
which are different kinds of business.

BIRDS OF THE AIR

#1228
Our heavenly Father is not merely the one from whom we originated. He is also the one caring and providing for us as we grow up.

#1229
Where Christ is exalted, He gathers the Church. Where the Church is exalted, it becomes a haunt for every unclean spirit, bird and beast.

#1230
However wayward the State becomes, the Church is the life in its veins. Its only escape from the work of the Spirit is found in self-harm.

#1231
Every attempt by man to create heaven on earth outside of submission to God (Catholicism, Communism, Secularism) results in hell on earth.

#1232
Scholarship has constructed a "veil of expertise," a hermeneutical industry which has alienated the West from the Bible just as Rome did.

#1233
If The West Wing were simply renamed The Messiah Complex it would instantly become brilliant satire.

#1234
If failed fathers invalidate patriarchy, medical malpractice invalidates hospitals.

GLORIFICATION

#1235
It is ironic that the "moral evolution" of Secularism quickly leads to cultural extinction.

#1236
Using "evolving" and "same-sex marriage" in the same sentence to describe a change of opinion merits a Darwin award.

#1237
The level of our understanding of the Bible is directly related to our willingness to learn the symbol language of God.

#1238
Polygamy began as a Cainite shortcut to dominion (many sons), the marriage equivalent of stealing fruit from the Tree of Knowledge.

#1239
Modern Bible scholars know the syntax of everything and the significance of nothing.

#1240
Secularism is supposedly a solid bookshelf upon which religions rest. But Christ is the shelf, and Secularism is just an empty book.

#1241
The secular square is simply the Church's front porch, Jesus' hospitality. Islam has no such front porch.

BIRDS OF THE AIR

#1242
Only a culture of human lemmings would pander to Islam
at home and fail to advocate for Christians abroad.

#1243
Cultural longevity requires a marriage of Church
and State. Secularism's "unmarried" states
will only decline and die childless.

#1244
Secular humanism and Islam are the bipolar moods of
Christless Christianity. They can be united only in suicide.

#1245
Europe is learning the hard way that a society not
driven by a central religious heart will find itself a
non-rejectable transplant.

#1246
True Christianity is peaceful, but Christians
are not necessarily so. True Islam is murderous,
but Muslims are not necessarily so.

#1247
The difference between Islam and Ebola
is that Ebola works faster.

#1248
Marriage promises a man some chamber music,
but through the years he should come to realize that
even one woman is an orchestra.

GLORIFICATION

#1249
Those who defile the springs of our culture
(Scripture, Church, Law, sacraments, marriage)
insist on drinking bottled water.

#1250
Medicine enabled Western culture to nip fatherlessness
in the bud. We reclassified orphans as abortions,
but they are still the fatherless.

#1251
When men are paternal, patriarchy works just fine.

#1252
Marriage can't be a sacrament because it is both
sacred and civil, a union of Church and State in one rite.

#1253
Modern Christians need to be up-to-speed on
philosophy only so we can deal with godless
philosophers in terms they can understand.

#1254
The Bible hasn't captured your imagination until
the imagined worlds of Lewis and Tolkien
look shallow and cheap.

#1255
If Mr. Goldsworthy understood "The Torah in Revelation"
instead of merely the Gospel, he might get a clue
as to what it's actually about.

BIRDS OF THE AIR

#1256
Secularism is just as bent on destroying centuries old cultural treasures as Islamic State, but far more subtle.

#1257
Something far worse than a millstone awaits the neck of every pro-abortion politician.

#1258
Lion and hive: Even in its death throes, the beastly old West ministers the honey of Canaan to the world.

#1259
People say and do unexpected things because there is a "subterranean logic" bubbling along under the surface. The Bible is just the same.

#1260
When God says that those who hate Him love death, He means non-Christians are on the wrong side of history.

#1261
The corruptocrats currently in power are the first generation which did not go to Sunday School.

#1262
Theology is the Church's invitation to "divide up" and take possession of the Bible. The very mind of God is part of our inheritance.

GLORIFICATION

#1263
At midnight, Boaz awoke from a deep sleep to discover the woman that the Lord had brought to him.

#1264
It's great to be excited about Jesus, but if you preach like you're not excited about the Bible, you might want to question your excitement.

#1265
So, the eternal God is involved—at great personal cost—in succession planning. Just imagine what's in store for us.

#1266
It's a good thing for our technologists that God doesn't patent his designs.

#1267
When it comes to Islam, progressives seem determined to live out the plot of "Mars Attacks."

#1268
Yes, we're Jesus' hands and feet in the world. But we're also His eyes, ears and nostrils. Charity requires prior discernment and judgment.

#1269
God didn't "rest and refresh" on Day 7 because He was tired. All music has rests. It's when you pause, breathe in and savor the work.

BIRDS OF THE AIR

#1270
It's time the chapter divisions were (mostly) removed from the Bible. They are a barrier to understanding the text.

#1271
Utopia is like the glory of Solomon. Try to build it and you become a tyrant. But submit to God and He will give it to you as a gift.

#1272
The historical-grammatical method is a lot like the Billings Method. Something passionate and fun is rendered sterile and mechanical.

#1273
A culture which rejects the fatherhood of God inevitably rejects fatherhood itself. Secularism is an orphanage run by delinquents.

#1274
Q: "How do I know if I'm a writer?"
A: "Do you write? If you write, you're a writer."

#1275
Israel's Feast of Booths continues today. Hospitality's open door is the heart of Jesus displayed in the Church.

#1276
The best political systems follow biblical principles. Yet the most unrighteous system would work if the people themselves were righteous.

GLORIFICATION

#1277
The Bible is eidetic. It thinks in pictures. Thinking in pictures is 1000 times faster than thinking in words.

#1278
People with Aspergers have always been with us.
In the old days, the monasteries were full of them.

#1279
If an Aspie is looking you in the eye,
he's probably assessing the level of pupil dilation.

#1280
Aspergers:
You small talk
But I'm oceans
Ecstasies, fears
And eardrum taut
A torrent dammed
By one-way eyes
Can't read you
Forgot your name.

#1281
Ideological stupidity is always the product of great but unconverted intelligence.

#1282
How about some separation between the Church of Secular Humanism and the State?

BIRDS OF THE AIR

#1283
Irreversible climate change?
The Vikings sailed across an ice-free Arctic Sea.
Never argue with a Viking.

#1284
What's the difference between secularists and lemmings?
At least lemmings procreate.

#1285
Instead of calling for better men, misguided feminism
turned women into men, resulting in less freedom
for women and children.

#1286
Women have been freed not from domineering men
but from womanhood.

#1287
Jesus never condemned same-sex marriage
because He wasn't into stating the obvious.

#1288
Same-sex marriage is an oxymoron because marriage
does not simply unite man and woman but confers the
offices of husband and wife.

#1289
Men successfully sold the idea to women that a
woman has no right to a husband/father but
instead has a right to kill her unborn child.

GLORIFICATION

#1290
Leftist thinking destroys because it pontificates on men, women, children, money and the environment with no idea of what they actually are.

#1291
Postmoderns love the words "sustainable" and "sexuality." But they won't allow anyone to marry them together. What bigots.

#1292
As we witness Europe's demise, perhaps it's time for a fornication tax. How big is your sexual footprint?

#1293
And man made marriage in his own image, and lobbied and bullied everyone, including God, to bless it and say that it was good.

#1294
The Woodstock generation is now running the USA. So rainbows will be ENFORCED.

#1295
The fundamental tenet of liberalism/progressivism is "We shall be gods."

#1296
The better I get to know the Word of Truth, the more the act of handling it feels like touching a live cable.

BIRDS OF THE AIR

#1297
How did you image God today, and to whom?

#1298
A jump to the Left always puts you in a timewarp.

#1299
There's one thing worse than children crying in church:
a church where there are no children.

#1300
Policing society is a bandaid. The root of the
problem is a crisis in fatherhood. We are paying
for police to be surrogate dads.

#1301
Same-sex marriage isn't another kind of apple just
waiting to be recognized. It's a worm in disguise.

#1302
Being buff and good in bed is just grandstanding of
potential. True virility is courage and godly offspring.

#1303
True progress in theology is understanding
the Bible better, not finding ways to
compromise with the secular zeitgeist.

#1304
The obvious answer to entertainment addiction
is supervised injecting rooms.

GLORIFICATION

#1305
The Bible is rejected in pursuit of sex & violence,
then rejected because it contains sex & violence.
And the Church is full of hypocrites?

#1306
Imagine a Bible commentary
where there were no notes at all,
just matrix icons
and indented margins in the Scripture.

#1307
The downside to working at home is that you're
always at home and always at work.

#1308
The e in eBook does not stand for elegant.

#1309
Only a culture where sex is divorced from
the future (procreation) could be so blind to the
long term cultural consequences of sexual sin.

#1310
The death of Western culture is merely
the pruning of the Church.

#1311
A million nihilistic road movies won't erase our
culture's memory of Bunyan's destination.

BIRDS OF THE AIR

#1312
The housing bubble and the college bubble are little bubbles on a much bigger bubble: Secularism.

#1313
Feminism tries and fails to make men useful by domesticating them. God makes them useful by dominating them.

#1314
Far better than possessing the countenance of an angel is the habitation of an ordinary face by an extraordinary moustache.

#1315
Feminism attempts and fails to domesticate a man. The Word of God does the opposite. It turns a man into a household.

#1316
Modern churches have replaced "dead formalism" with a sort of undead formlessness.

#1317
Warhol iconized celebrities using ink and paint. Now we have politicians that are nothing but ink and paint. Politics has been Warholized.

#1318
Reading the Bible typologically is not a rejection of historical truth. It is an acceptance that history is shaped by a single Author.

GLORIFICATION

#1319
"Here am I, and the children God has given me."
Only through Church history can the Son learn
what it is to be the Father.

#1320
Democracy was intended for the purpose of choosing
good stewards, not for voting on what is truth.

#1321
If marriage is the backbone of a society, it's little wonder
our own culture is increasingly spineless.

#1322
We live in a culture desperate to maintain the blessings
of Christianity but without the Christ.

#1323
The "insanity" of the faithful is eventually vindicated.
The wisdom of the unfaithful is shown to be bankrupt.

#1324
We complained about two dimensional heroes and villains
so Hollywood gave us 3D movies.

#1325
Any dumb person can swallow a dumb idea,
but it takes an academic to swallow a really big dumb idea.

#1326
So many Pastor-tweets sound like they were written by
Sphinx from the movie Mystery Men.

BIRDS OF THE AIR

#1327
The Revelation is a mystery, yet it is also
a book composed almost entirely of clues.

#1328
Revelation recapitulates Israel's feasts.
Booths is about Satan being bound from gathering the
nations while Jesus gathers them.

#1329
Jargon starts out as way to encapsulate and
communicate big ideas and ends as a means
of excluding people. A bit like TEDtalks.

#1330
Thanks to some magnificent legislation,
progressive culture is now without sin.
Everyone's a victim. No one's a perp.

#1331
Hermeneutics isn't an autopsy.
It's a long-running forensic crime show.

#1332
This is an age when the time and effort spent
talking about how to interpret the Bible
totally eclipses the time and effort spent doing it.

#1333
Hermeneutics is like sex. Everyone is talking about it or
perverting it, but hardly anybody is actually doing it.

GLORIFICATION

#1334
It is ironic that our culture developed incredible means of delivering content right when it finally had nothing worthwhile left to say.

#1335
What's worse than a culture enslaved to darkness? A culture with unparalleled knowledge of God which willfully invents a new darkness.

#1336
Racial equality in the USA should have been framed in terms of "responsibilities" instead of "rights." Now everyone's a victim.

#1337
The best leaders are not those with perfect policy but those with strength and integrity. Character covers a multitude of policy foibles.

#1338
Catatonia sounds like a nice place for a short break.

#1339
The secular state denies the reality of sin and is then shocked when sins grow to become crimes.

#1340
Secular humanism is deficient in that it has no definition of "sin." All that's left to statists is "crime."

BIRDS OF THE AIR

#1341
Secular humanism is the kind of humanism which has no regard for past humans, future humans, inconvenient humans, or non-secular humans.

#1342
The Old Covenant was about mercy: bringing the debt to zero. The New is about grace: filling our accounts with glory.

#1343
The redefinition of marriage is a hijacking of its good name in order to coerce a blessing upon that which is cursed.

#1344
Every Bible text is a precise "mathematical" formula. Sadly, even the best modern theology boils down to "Oh look, there's another x."

#1345
Somebody please explain to Americans what classless society actually means.

#1346
As champions of personal freedom, secularists are surprisingly preachy.

#1347
Progressives destroy the future, so Conservatives try to recreate the past. What we need are true Progressives: postmillennial Christians.

GLORIFICATION

#1348
When the State usurps the Church, pragmatism replaces prayer, policy replaces doctrine, and sins become crimes.

#1349
The Green movement is against forestry, farming and family, that is, all forms of husbandry. It seems Gaia is condemned to be a spinster.

#1350
Modern theology tries to distill the Bible into something precise. But symbols are precise and nothing is less precise than modern theology.

#1351
Reading a book about theology is like watching a movie about Hollywood.

#1352
Sometimes, the best way to shed new light on a theological debate is to put aside its history and its factions.

#1353
Gay isn't the new black. It's a slavery to sin, and they are not lobbying to be released.

#1354
"Community services" are atheism's failed attempt at community. Stop whining and get back to Church, where you have to pay it forward.

BIRDS OF THE AIR

#1355
Secularism is a prodigal brat intent on squandering
its inheritance – 2000 years of Christian culture –
on "riotous living."

#1356
God's answer to privilege and exploitation in society is love.
Man's answer is to privilege the underprivileged
and exploit the exploiters.

#1357
True hospitality not only feeds,
it also instructs and "bears children."

#1358
It was a relief to find out God likes parties.
Evangelism is obedience, fasting, prayer, suffering,
witness, generosity AND PARTIES.

#1359
Heaven is a party.
Getting in depends on who you know.

#1360
Based on Hebrews 6:1-3, I'd say we are still in the early
Church. We don't even have the basics down yet.

> "The public is against you
> but the future is yours."

— SERGEI SHCHUKIN TO MATISSE

Made in the USA
Middletown, DE
09 May 2018